KU-661-037

THE CROSSING

A STORY OF EAST TIMOR

LUÍS CARDOSO

TRANSLATED FROM THE PORTUGUESE BY
MARGARET JULL COSTA

Foreword by
Jill Jolliffe

GALWAY COUNTY LIBRARIES

Granta Books
London

Granta Publications, 2/3 Hanover Yard, London N1 8BE

First published in Portugal as *Crónica de uma travessia: A época do Ai-Dik-Funam*, Publicações Dom Quixote, 1997.
First published in English in Great Britain by Granta Books 2000.

Copyright © 1997 by Luís Cardoso.
Translation copyright © 2000 by Margaret Jull Costa.
Foreword © 2000 by Jill Jolliffe.

Luís Cardoso has asserted his moral right under the Copyright, Designs and Patents Act, 1988, to be identified as the author of this work.

All rights reserved. No reproduction, copy or transmissions of this publication may be made without written permission.
No paragraph of this publication may be reproduced, copied or transmitted save with written permission or in accordance with the provisions of the Copyright Act 1956 (as amended). Any person who does any unauthorized act in relation to this publication may be liable to criminal prosecution and civil claims for damages.

A CIP catalogue record for this book
is available from the British Library.

13 5 7 9 10 8 6 4 2

ISBN 1 86207 352 X

Typeset in Sabon by M Rules
Printed and bound in Great Britain
by Mackays of Chatham plc

TRANSLATOR'S ACKNOWLEDGEMENTS

I would like to thank Ben Ball, Luísa Campos, Martin Jenkins, Manucha Lisboa and John G. Taylor for all their help and advice, and, in particular, the author, Luís Cardoso.

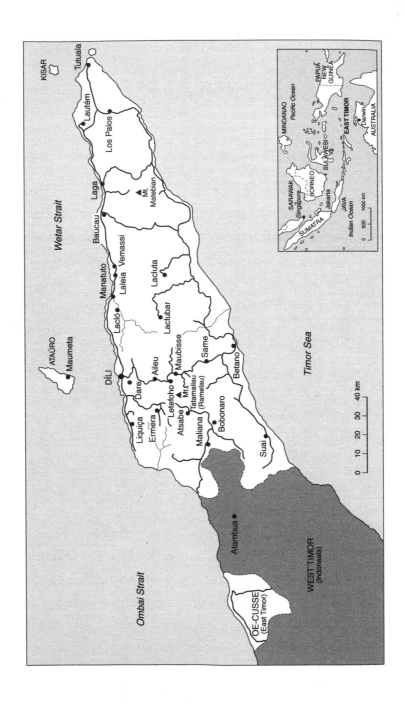

FOREWORD

Luís Cardoso's *The Crossing* is a story of change, of
transition from one state and time to another, an East
Timorese personal odyssey told at the time the author's
homeland is in the throes of its greatest transition: to
nationhood, after four centuries of Portuguese colonial
occupation and 24 years of Indonesian military occupation. It does not aim to be a political book in the narrow
sense, although like all good books it is in the deepest
sense, but is the memoir of a Timorese childhood which
spans this recent period of national captivity. It is the
first work of creative prose to be published by an East
Timorese writer in modern times, and is as much set in a
timeless Timorese spirit world, not unlike the Australian
Aboriginal dreamtime, as it is in the contemporary real
world.

Cardoso went to Lisbon as a young forestry student
before Portugal's revolution of April 25th, 1974. When
the new government's decolonization programme paved
the way for the Indonesian invasion instead of bringing
the freedom it promised, it left him separated from his
homeland, family and friends, condemned to a period

of enforced exile that was only to end in late
1999, when UN troops entered East Timor after the
country's vote for independence. One of the few things
he retained was his nickname: he had been dubbed
'Takas' (high heels) by his classmates because of the
stylish Cuban heels he sported in the heady days pre-
ceding the Portuguese revolution, when Díli
trend-setters grew their hair into wild Afro halos and
sent out to the Chinese tailor for Guevara-style guerrilla suits. Another was his political consciousness – he
is a member of East Timor's leading National Council
for Timorese Resistance. For many Timorese, exiled
before or after the Indonesian invasion, these were the
few things they had: their language, their stories and
their desire for independence.

There are many crossings in the book – Takas's
crossing from childhood to manhood under the watchful
eye of the Jesuits; a childhood sea crossing from the capital Díli to Ataúro island, traditional seat of banishment
under the dictatorship of António de Oliveira Salazar; his
crossing into a life of exile after he is stranded in Lisbon;
and the final crossing from life to death of his father, the
event which frames the book. Many of these crossings
are by water, which is ever-present in the text and in the
Timorese consciousness. There is the sea, inextricably
linked with the Portuguese imperial adventure, and
Lisbon's Tagus river – studied in schoolbooks which

told the boy nothing of his own land, but which he later came to cross daily by ferry; there are the coursing torrents which criss-cross the East Timorese countryside, and the two seas, *tassi-mane* and *tassi-feto*, the wild 'male' sea of the south coast and the gentle 'female' sea of the north coast, which define the Timorese physical world.

The effect of the elements on the Timorese outlook is intensely spiritual, however. Early in the book, Takas's family makes a night journey from Díli, the capital of Timor, to Ataúro island, through rough seas in a fragile boat. His mother orders Takas to keep watch as others sleep in case the sea plays a trick on them ('a *tassi-fila*, with the waves turning inside out'). As the passengers' stories are revealed, so is their common humanity and the importance of the forces of magic. The ancient helmsman tells of his family tragedy which has bound him to a life at sea, ferrying lost souls between the mainland and the island. Tuna and sharks guide the boat; when Simão, a prisoner, leans overboard to wash his face, a long, white shark comes up to meet him, stopping inches away. An ancestor, says the helmsman, come to meet you; the people of Ataúro are never attacked by sharks. These are links which must be respected, and cannot be severed, no matter which dictatorship rules the island.

In animist belief the dead coexist with the living and

the borders between the visible and invisible world
are ill-defined – it is sometimes necessary to resort to
magic to resolve immediate problems and restore the
equilibrium of the universe. But exile breaks this rich,
sustaining spiritual network. In one of the book's most
moving passages, Cardoso gets lost in the Lisbon sub-
urbs with two other Timorese. Domingos and Mau
Mali come from a very different background from
Cardoso, rural labourers from the western border area
of Bobonaro who washed up on Lisbon's shores in
1976 as refugees from the Indonesian invasion and
are now working on a construction site. They bring
comfort, humour and a touch of Timorese magic to
the burgeoning young intellectual. When the bus they
catch one night to the refugee neighbourhood of
Odivelas takes them in the wrong direction, Mau
Mali resorts to the *rain-fila* ritual as a logical and natural remedy to their distress, putting his clothes on
back-to-front, to fool the spirit which has tried to trick
them. They eventually get back to their lodging, but
whether they will ever really find their way home
remains to be seen.

This sense of the exile's spiritual dislocation domi-
nates Cardoso's Lisbon sections, stemming from the
strangeness of their environment, the longing for a distant homeland that is closed to them, hermetically sealed
from the world, and anxiety over the fate of loved ones

held hostage by the Indonesian military. For the Lisbon community and other Timorese of the diaspora, the years 1975 to 1999, particularly the earlier years, were marked by a trickle of information – in the form of smuggled letters, photos, and personal accounts of the lucky few who managed to escape – telling of unspeakable crimes committed on a daily basis by the Indonesian military: bombings, executions, torture and disappearances, which left no family untouched. East Timor was not then the fashionable cause it is today, and the exiles suffered alone. The advancing dementia of Takas's dying father is the most eloquent testimony to the malaise. As the text cuts between Portugal and Timor, the alienation of those who have escaped to Lisbon makes a poignant, ambiguous contrast to the author's childhood of rural innocence, albeit lived under an oppressive colonial regime.

In this isolated, confined community, political activity tended to turn in on itself. In his first years in the Portuguese capital the young exile shared the company of other homesick nationalists from Portugal's colonies, such as Angola's Agostinho Neto and Guinea Bissau's Amílcar Cabral, the admired theoretician of anti-colonialism and an ideological father to the Timorese. Lisbon's melancholic spirit infects the émigrés who, like the Russians in the Geneva of Joseph Conrad's *Under Western Eyes*, enter into endless political

intrigues which tend to devour the conspirators and
defeat the aims they work for, as factions and internal
rivalries multiply.

This sense of psychological desolation is offset by
Takas's ironic wit and amusing pen sketches of his
contemporaries in the 1960s, many of whom will soon
form East Timor's first independent government. He
pokes fun at them but is quite devoid of malice – the
humour is self-mocking, because Cardoso shares the
same origins.

One of the major influences Cardoso has in common
with most of this new generation of East Timorese leaders
is their education by Jesuit priests, whose influence per-
vades the book. Not all had a vocation for the priesthood,
but higher education was available only to a tiny elite,
through church missions; most took the education and
passed on the priesthood, often to the disappointment of
their parents. This strange breed of other-worldly young
men makes a strong impression on the young Cardoso,
and eventually he takes a place amongst them in the Jesuit
seminary at Dare, in the cool, leafy hills overlooking Díli.
This 'eagle's nest' has a special place in Timorese hearts, as
a seat of learning and a beacon of freedom in difficult
times. In the Salazar era it was a retreat beyond the reach
of the dreaded PIDE, the Portuguese secret police, where
freedom of the mind and spirit remained inviolate. The
friendships and political groups formed by the students

there in the sixties were to play a decisive role in East Timor's future. Elsewhere, students of the world were experimenting with new lifestyles, marching in the streets to end the war in Vietnam, and calling for a new social order. Portugal and its colonies lived cut off from the rest of the world, with censorship ensuring they knew very little of this: the study groups of Dare were the only possible equivalent, an important crucible of nationalist thought. During the long black night of the Indonesian occupation, the seminary was bombed savagely, but European Jesuit priests refused the easy option of repatriation and stood by the Timorese with great courage.

I first visited what was then Portuguese Timor in April 1975. I had never been outside my native Australia before and it was a journey that was to leave an indelible impression on me, indeed to change my life forever: it was a 'crossing' in the deepest sense.

There were two factors that contributed to this forceful impression. The first was the sheer physical beauty of East Timor and its people and the second was the infectious mood of hope and happiness that reigned. This exotic land invaded my senses from the first moment I saw its great mist-wreathed cordillera looming out of the sea. Our tiny plane circled over the whitewashed city of Díli, bounced along its dirt airstrip scattering pigs

and buffalo, and delivered us to a vast waiting crowd
which claimed us as its own. We were a mixed delega-
tion of trade unionists, students and parliamentarians
(I was of the second group), judged to be harbingers of
change and as such given a royal welcome. We were
escorted by Timorese warriors mounted on small ponies,
proud and resplendent in brilliantly-coloured woven
cloths, with sabres hanging in ornate sheaths and bejew-
elled horsehair decorating their ankles. There was an
elusive sweet scent which I identify to this day with the
special nature of that Timor experience. It clung in the
thick tropical air, mingled with the sweat of the hundreds of Timorese bodies pressing against us, and
recurred at unexpected times during the rest of our visit.

These physical sensory impressions, strong as they
were, were secondary to the intense psychological mood.
The dictatorship in Portugal had fallen only a year
before, and for the first time in modern history the East
Timorese believed they were in reach of freedom.
Although they were Australia's nearest neighbours,
we knew next to nothing about them. They had been
muzzled for the best part of a century and now they
were reaching out – they wanted to know everything
about us and what was happening in the outside world,
to exchange knowledge. Their generous, unbounded
hospitality stemmed from this innocent openness, a
willing embrace of other cultures, which eight months

later was to be poisoned at the source by the Indonesian invasion. Balanced between Portuguese decolonization and Indonesian occupation, the East Timorese were experiencing a brief taste of democracy, and it was a moment like no other in their history.

I returned several months later and became, almost by accident, Reuters correspondent in Díli, and a witness to the historic period between civil war and Jakarta's invasion which stretched from August to December 1975. I marched with nationalist guerrillas, who trod the cordillera with the ease and speed of mountain goats, learning that the only way to keep up was to place my foot exactly in the footstep of the person ahead; I had my baptism of fire in a cross-border mortar attack at Batugade, was strafed by a Mitchell B26 bomber at Atabae and had the sad task of reporting the deaths of five of my colleagues at the border town of Balibo, shot down as they attempted to report the Indonesian advance. Through these experiences my life became inextricably entwined with the lives of the Timorese, and almost with the soil of that land that became so dear to me.

Like Luís Cardoso, I spent a period of exile in Portugal, although his was enforced and mine was elected. In Lisbon I could live close to the East Timorese refugee community and distant from the many Australians and their duplicitous leaders who seemed to have forgotten their human duty. During my years based there scraping a living as a writer, for the *Guardian*, BBC and others, I travelled widely and saw other wars first hand, in Angola and the western Sahara, gaining experience and strength for the day I would return. When a Polisario Front guerrilla jokingly offered me his Kalashnikov to fire off a round into the desert, as others of our press group had done, I thought sadly of the East Timorese and declined. War here seemed like a game: the Saharawis had a luxurious flow of arms from neighbouring Algeria, whereas for the Timorese each bullet was a precious commodity stolen or scrounged from their enemy, to be treasured and used only when the right opportunity offered itself.

Nineteen years passed before I returned to Timor again. It was a joyous, but illegal and difficult homecoming. Once again I placed my feet in the footsteps of the guerrillas, who led me by night to Commander Nino Konis Santana, but things went badly wrong and I also saw the grim inside of an Indonesian military prison. The Timorese were then four years from their eventual political freedom, and many, including Konis, were still to die at the hands of the occupation army, but my contact with the resistance was growing closer once again, as though a cycle was drawing to a close.

Works of East Timorese literature marked the beginning and end of this cycle. In December 1975, as Indonesian forces closed in on the East Timorese capital,

I was asked to carry out of the territory a small manuscript of poems written by Francisco Borja da Costa, a contemporary of Luís Cardoso's who had also studied in Lisbon. I reached Darwin with this precious parcel a few days before Indonesian paratroopers assaulted the capital. His work was saved, but he was not: he was publicly executed by an Indonesian firing squad just a few days after he handed the work to me.

His work represented the beginning of a new self-conscious phase of cultural revival, but it was also the beginning of Timor's longest nightmare. During their 24-year struggle for liberation the Timorese always considered their culture as one of their weapons, and Indonesia's failure to subjugate these courageous people was as much due to their profound sense of their own cultural identity as their unrelenting military resistance.

The last Indonesian soldiers withdrew from Díli in September 1999, after the East Timorese population had voted overwhelmingly for independence in a UN-sponsored referendum a month earlier, and after a last round of unmatched brutality. From the ashes a new country is emerging. The healing process will take many years, and will be inseparable from cultural growth; from it, a new literature will emerge, whether in the Portuguese or Tetum language. As the first work to be published in English in the post-Indonesian era, *The Crossing* is in the vanguard of that cultural renaissance. Francisco Borja da

Costa, a gentle friend whose only crime was to live in the world of ideas, set it in motion; twenty-five years later Luís Cardoso has continued his work, opening a small window onto that special mix of spirituality, interaction with nature and proud sense of identity which makes up the East Timorese universe.

Jill Jolliffe, Darwin, April 2000

I

It was a hot Thursday in the month of June 1990. I crossed the river by boat as I did every morning. A habit I had acquired in order to savour an old familiar pleasure. On that day, I was dressed all in white, cool and immaculate, newly emerged from a cold water bath, just as I had been when he led me to the altar to receive my first communion. The jacaranda trees had filled Lisbon with their liturgical purple in celebration of the return of the heat and an end to the days of sleep and darkness. The doctors had promised that he would be home by the end of the week, although they might as well have said the end of the day, or of the morning, or of time itself. On the way to the hospital, my mother – taking care not to show me her true feelings – said she had been told in a dream that he had gathered his belongings together and departed. Her face was serene, as if to say that he was serene too, but beads of sweat stood out on her forehead, in sympathy with his final climb up the sacred mountain. This time he would not be coming back down again to the city of Díli. He had grown tired and was resting.

Days before, the police had found him wandering the streets of Seixal, the town across the Tagus from Lisbon. They said he was speaking in a strange language and seemed to be looking for someone. When he got home, he told us he had been to the town of Betano, on the south coast of Timor; he was searching for a distant relative he had known during the war, but the place looked different now – its inhabitants had disappeared and the houses were all painted white and occupied by Portuguese people, *malaes*, who couldn't speak Mambae.

He had arrived in Portugal four years before, along with his family, to recover the memory he had lost in a car accident in Díli after coming back from the bush. He had come hoping to find his due reward, not so much in payment for the years he spent as a committed and diligent servant of the empire but for the way they, the Timorese people, had risen to the task of standing in for the distant motherland during her absence in troubled times.

He was a member of the UDT (Timorese Democratic Union) and a committed defender of *mate-bandera-hum*, a Tetum expression meaning 'to die in the shadow of the Portuguese flag'. As such, he was imprisoned by Fretilin (Revolutionary Front of Independent East Timor) during the civil war that followed the flight of his party's leaders. He said that although he had been badly treated –

which was only to be expected, given what happened to Fretilin militants in the hands of his fellow UDT members, who then took refuge across the border under the protection of a different flag – he had forgotten all his old enmities while in captivity and in daily contact with the young people there. Some of them were more communist than others, the priests of supreme ideals in the vestments of guerrillas, some more sacrificed than sacrificing, but all were prepared to give their lives for the cause and had vowed to win back the land promised by their dead. He wept whenever he remembered their faces and their names, which irritated old Clara; she had stayed behind in the city and would ask him jokingly if his tears were for the life of ease he had led in the comforting arms of the *bibere*, the woman he had left behind in the bush. He would retort that just as two wars were one war too many, so two women were too much comfort for one man. The Japanese had gone, and now the Indonesians were there. No one knew when they would go. His belief in *mate-bandera-hum* held firm, and he felt a legitimate and inalienable right to demand the return of the Portuguese, so that Portugal could recover her memory of motherhood, and the Timorese the memory of their birth.

He was my father and the descendant of families from Manufahi, a land whose name bespoke terror and betrayal. He had followed the route taken by many

young men from the south coast who – once hearts and
hostilities had been pacified, the rebellious local ruler, or
liurai, vanquished, and the redemption of his subjects
obtained – had gone to study at the school in Soibada,
founded by priests in 1898 to train catechism teachers as
missionaries. The school was largely attended by the
sons of local rulers who, once removed from their native,
independent environments and classified as educated,
became instruments for spreading the language, culture
and religion of Portugal.

The school lay behind buttressed walls in a dank,
muddy place near Samoro, and looked out over the
magnificent Aitara hill, which was surrounded by
bamboo groves and topped by a chapel built on the spot
where Our Lady was said to have appeared. Samoro had
surrendered to both the charms and the weapons of the
intellectual and aristocratic elite of the Lacló kingdom,
whose leader, Dom Luís dos Reis de Noronha, was
raised to the rank of brigadier, declared a national hero
and placed on the same pedestal as various other heroes
from the mother country for having been the right-hand
man of the then governor of East Timor, Filomeno da
Câmara, in the pacification of the territory and the
defeat of the local ruler Dom Boaventura of Manufahi,
who had rebelled in 1912. The official historians attrib-
uted the revolt to the bad character and bellicose
instincts of that rebellious *liurai*, who refused to pay

levies and taxes to the region's protector. The governor used this as a pretext for finally putting an end to the privileges hitherto enjoyed by the traditional authorities, a policy aided by the demise of the monarchy in Portugal, which had been the patron and protector of native power.

My father confided to me that the stories and rumours going round the villages, and particularly those told by his protector and godfather, Mário de Noronha, son-in-law to the late Dom Boaventura, identified a different origin to hostilities. They said that the Queen of Manufahi, Dom Boaventura's wife, was very pale and very pretty, and that her beauty was a torment to the military commander of Same, Álvares da Silva, who coveted her and, even though he was married and had a son, fell totally under her spell. He, a soldier and guardian of the sacred interests of the motherland and of the Nation's closest secrets, intended to rescue her from a marriage which he believed to be against nature and contrary to the Portuguese policy of keeping white skins and dark skins separate. Such passion and daring cost him dear, for he paid with his life for the anger of the tribal chief, the woman's husband.

My father did not become a catechism teacher. When he had finished his primary education, he went back to Same. While waiting to begin his nursing course, he became a coffee-grower and married my mother, who was from Fahinihan and spoke Laclei. A priest from the Azores gave them a gift – a kerosene lamp, which would accompany the family's peregrinations around the island, lighting up both my home and the roads that my father walked at night, following the sighs of the dying and the groans of women in labour, as he went about his work as a professional recoverer of lives. But for me, that hooded lamp (which looked like a prelate dressed in white, wearing a pith helmet) was the best present I was ever given, albeit indirectly, for that well of light illuminated my childhood as I made my first shaky attempts at writing the letters of the alphabet, as I formed my first words and wrote my first compositions in the company of bats, owls and other strange, extravagant creatures whom the light attracted from far away on the island, from the depths of the earth and the seas, from the horizon of my dreams and my nightmares, to perch on the window sill, eyes wide, astonished at my intrusive presence there. They began to appear in the plots of my compositions, frightening my primary school teacher, who talked to my father about it, and prompted him to arrange individual catechism lessons for me and a rapid, compulsory first communion.

My father was called to begin his nursing course just as the Second World War broke out. When the Japanese entered Timor, he was already supplying arms to the Australian commandos, who were engaged in an intense, uneven battle with the Japanese. The war left him with scars which he wore like medals and which, with a certain modesty, he kept covered up; he also had many stories to relate, as well as the names of the Australian soldiers he had helped, names which, before his death, he bequeathed to me, urging me to claim some form of recompense. He religiously kept empty cartridge cases as trophies of war and would hang them from the ceiling of my apartment to ward off the evil eye, demons and burglars. Then, when he heard my mother humming the melancholy, monotonous songs she had learned from the soldiers of the Empire of the Rising Sun when she was held hostage by the Japanese in the village of Ulfu, he would start singing songs in English, and then it was as if the war continued in my own house, as if, in their minds, it had never really ended. All in all, more than 50,000 Timorese died, guaranteeing Portugal the continuance of its tragic colonial adventure, and guaranteeing the Australians the present sovereignty of Her Majesty the Queen. In exchange, we were left with the wreckage of a few planes on land and about the same number of rusting, battered hulks which are still rotting in the Timorese seas, giving Timor's inhabitants something to rest their weary eyes on while they wait for help. Meanwhile, in the skies, the vultures drank toasts in champagne to the treaty that gave them the right to suck up from the high seas the *mina-rai*, the fat of the land: oil.

He returned to his nursing course and, when he graduated, was sent to do his internship in the frontier regions, in that land of cattle rustlers who would take refuge on either side of the border, depending on the monsoons and who was after them at the time. On horseback, beneath the haughty gaze of the *kuda-uluns**, he travelled the towns of Bobonaro – Marobo and its hot springs, Cailaco and its stone fort, Maliana and its vast plain – always accompanied by his box of syringes, and always on the trail of malaria, typhoid and dysentery. Quite often he had to sew up the gaping wounds of some smuggler who had been foolish enough to go to sleep with a buffalo tethered to his ankle, a buffalo filched from a corral owned by one of the local wealthy, well-defended aristocracy.

I was born on a day when, returning home to Cailaco, he was waylaid by a rustler who asked only for his protection and his silence. The man's name was Landa, and he claimed to be from a far-off island which he had fled after killing his wife's kidnapper; he had then crossed the sea in search of the border and another flag to shelter him. He was a teacher of *silat*, the martial art of which Sandokan, a hero of popular fiction, was an eminent exponent. Officially, he was a cattle dealer, but he had no roof over his head, far less a flag, and had lost his cattle,

---

* A pejorative term used to describe people from the Bobonaro region of East Timor.

his wife and an eye in sundry battles. He was charged
with taking care of me and with teaching my father *silat*
and other magical arts by the light of the full moon.
Two years later, I was baptized at the administrative post
of Laclubar where my father, the novice nurse, had been
transferred. Under the influence of the wizard Landa,
he had added to his skills that of medicine man for those
illnesses beyond the reach of penicillin. This was near
Soibada and its school, and near the wells of natural gas
at Pualaka and the eternal flames that emerged from
inside the earth. The family kerosene lamp was fuelled
for free by oil from that well. Old Landa did not come
with us, because he felt safer near the no-man's-land that
others called the border.

Teachers from the Soibada school would visit our
house – patients or relatives or former colleagues of my
father. They would smile and drop their trousers for an
injection, and I was told that, one day, I would be given
over to their educational care. They would pull up their
trousers again, looking pained, and listen enthusiasti-
cally while my father proudly listed their names, which,
to me, rang out like so many bamboo canes thwacking
across my buttocks, which ached as if from multiple,
painful penicillin injections. There they were, lined up
and waiting for me at the school in Soibada.

We received the order to leave cold, windy Laclubar,
where they grew tea, strawberries and persimmons and

drank buffalo milk, and, with our belongings and the kerosene lamp packed, we travelled down in the rain from the Cribas tableland, our horses skidding on the muddy paths. I noticed how silent my parents were, as if carrying a heavy burden or about to undergo some painful punishment or penance. The river valley of Lacló spread out like a vast plain, flanked by ricefields. (Later, a local governor would try to prolong his reign by ordering a bridge named after him to be built, in imitation of the mother country, but the rebellious, unruly waters of the monsoons took it upon themselves to reduce the bridge to a pile of rubble – a warning of things to come.) Dark buffaloes slept in the rectangular fields and the barechested men who worked the fields had heavy, swollen legs caused by a disease rife in the flooded rice paddies, a disease my father called elephantiasis, in Tetum *ain-potes*, which I took to mean that they had feet the shape of boots.

In Manatuto, an old Chevrolet awaited us, which the driver soon cranked up. Then the car set off, grunting and sweating, over the parched, stony hills of Subão, in which, beneath the dense woods of white gum trees, the Indonesians later discovered a rich seam of marble to exploit. On every bend there was a little chapel, the figure of a saint or an admonitory white cross bearing the name of someone who had died. My mother made the driver stop at each place so that she could say a prayer and thus prevent us meeting the same fate as those who had plummeted over the precipice bristling with razor-sharp rocks, down into the calm, blue sea full of waiting sharks.

There were no lights on in Díli when we were deposited on Lecidere beach, near the Bishop's palace. We went to see the bishop, Dom Jaime Garcia Goulart, who gave us his blessing, and to this day I do not know if he did so because he felt sorry for my family in particular or for all those whose profession sends them into enforced exile. On the beach, my anxious mother lit the kerosene lamp and walked the whole length of the sands, lighting up the sea in search of the *beiro* that would take us to the island of Ataúro, visible hunched in the pitch-dark night like a giant turtle which, in search of immortality, had turned itself into land. I was afraid the boat might lose its way in the night, buffeted by arbitrary winds and counter-currents, and follow another star off in a different direction, to a different destination.

Our family solitude was soon broken by the arrival of an African *cipaio*, the descendant of former deportees from Mozambique, the famous Landins, now employed as dogs of war and pacifiers of native uprisings. I could only see his white teeth and hear his gruff, loud voice, as he laughed and gave embarkation orders to a prisoner, either a political prisoner or a common criminal – at the time it came to the same thing, for they all shared the same destination and fate.

Once on board, I saw the *sokão*, the steersman, close to for the first time. He looked tiny on land, but on the sea he was impressive. He was the captain of the broad, flat boat. He wore only a loincloth or *hakfolik* – a tiny piece of clothing appropriate for someone who spends his life between sea and sky. He sat down in the stern, and, just as the lights in the city came on, picked up a white conch shell. Putting the shell to his lips, he tilted it as if it were full of *tua-akar*, palm wine, as if he wanted to drink it all down to sweeten bitter crossings. Instead he blew, and a long, languid sound emerged, a call for some supernatural being to fill the sails with a good following wind to carry us across to the island. The sailors sang as they rowed,

Héan ró, ró berabera
Bá ne'e bé, bá Manukoko.

The African, whose name was Aldroado, blew the white foam off his real palm wine and tore at some dried fish with his teeth; then he put his hands into the water to wash them, but also perhaps to assure himself that the sea provided as solid a barrier as any prison walls. He shook off the drops of water, wrapped himself in a sarong and asked, 'When do we arrive?'

'Tomorrow.'

'Tomorrow! Does your clock tell the time by days rather than hours?'

His booming laugh frightened my mother.

'Tomorrow it is, then!' he said and went to sleep.

My family did the same. I remained on watch to give the alarm should the boat head off in another direction. I had heard stories of travellers who had lost their way because of a *rain-fila*, a trick the land plays on intruders, turning everything around and obliging the travellers to resort to trickery too, getting their guide to remove all his clothes and put them on again back to front in order to find the path home. On the sea such a trick would be called a *tassi-fila*, with the waves turning inside out, causing a shipwreck that would drag everything down to the ocean depths. No tricks could save us then.

My mother was also on the alert.

'You keep watch, child.'

The prisoner, Simão, remained silent, staring back at the mountains. He took a deep breath, inhaling the scent of his homeland hidden far away amongst the mountains. He did not know when he would go back or, indeed, if he had any hope of ever returning. He lowered his gaze to the city itself. Lights illuminated the coast road, perhaps merely for the benefit of spirits leaving their mean little rooms to wander the empty spaces. A troupe of dogs chased after something, barking. The city was otherwise immersed in the silence of men. Simão listened to the sound of that silence. The sound of people falling asleep. Magnificent and terrifying, as at the very beginning or at the very end of time. He took off his sandals and held them in his hand. He wanted to see the face of the big land as he said goodbye to it. To see if it was laughing at him, weeping for him or about to kill him. He had always been afraid of what might be going on behind his back, even if it were only a caress. That is why he looked the city straight in the eye. And the city shrank shyly into a brilliant line skirting the bay. Distant.

The old steersman did not want to speak to Simão. He was watching him. But I realized that he felt a great desire to console and protect him, as if he himself were the island, our destination.

The steersman had made other crossings with other exiles, but he had never felt drawn to them as he did to Simão. And that was due mainly to Simão's contemplative silence, an infectious silence that reminded him of his son, Lamartinho, who had left his own island some time before in order to go to school in Maliana, and who had then returned to become head of the *suku** in Maquili. And Simão was calmed by the presence of the old man, although, despite the rolling waves that sometimes blocked his view, he kept his eyes fixed on the lights. When he could no longer make out the details of

---

* A princedom converted under Portuguese rule into an administrative unit.

the city, he looked at the lights approaching the boat, the gleaming eyes of the fish, the young tuna and the sharks that rubbed against the wooden hull. Then the steersman saw his face fill with fear, saw all the tumult of his life descend upon him, contorting his face, unsettling his gaze, his eyes calling out for some human presence, some urgent help, some *terra firma* like the one he had left behind.

'It's all right,' said the old man.

Simão started at this interruption to his thoughts. The old man's voice fanned out beneath Simão's gaze like a ship's wake.

'They're less dangerous than men. They know everything. They're the ones who guide the boat. They follow the sea currents. We learn how to navigate from them.'

The old man fell silent again. The sailors had just dragged up a young shark and now were returning it to the sea, an action that would doubtless be rewarded later on. It was said that no native of Ataúro had ever been attacked by a shark, unless he or she was under a curse or had offended some custom, creature or ancestor. The men's silence signified their contrition for their mistake. Simão had not even noticed them fishing.

When the creatures of the sea once more nuzzled the ship's hull, the old man spoke again.

'I prefer to sail at night. I can find my way more easily. Sometimes, when I have to carry an angry passenger, the sea grows wild. Nature mirrors men's feelings. When I saw you on the beach,' – the old man stopped speaking in order to remember – 'I knew at once that, with you on board, the sea would grow calm. I feel sorry for him over there,' indicating the sleeping African with a lift of his chin, 'not even the weather takes any notice of him. How old are you?'

'Not yet old enough to be considered old.'

'That old, eh? As for me, my boy,' he paused and gave a dispirited sigh, 'I've spent more of my life on the sea than on the land.'

'Don't you ever get tired of it?' asked Simão, turning around.

'You only get tired of the sea if all you see is water. Sometimes,' – he looked round as if to gauge the weather – 'I get caught up in violent storms. When I reach land again, I find palm trees and coconut palms torn out by the roots, the earth churned up and the grainstores, the *manlekas*, blown out of the trees. Sometimes I sail right through a waterspout, right through the colours of the rainbow. What comforts me is that, after the storm, the sea is as tame as the tuna that come and take food from my hands.'

Simão hunched over his knees and closed his eyes. He wanted to fall asleep to the sound of the old man's voice.

'I want you to see the sunrise over the sea,' said the old man. 'You can barely notice the sunset. It's so quick you scarcely have time to see it. It's just a fraction of a second which only certain people catch. Go to sleep if you like. I'll wake you when it's time.'

The old man watched him settle down, first clasping his legs in his arms, then resting his head on his knees. He didn't fall asleep at once; he needed time for his body to become used to the rhythm of the boat, of the currents, of the sea. He would have to forget the pulse of the land and slowly enter the rhythm of the waves. Some men, like the old steersman, wear the marks of the waves on their skin. Big waves at first, that grow smaller when they meet other waves. Then, when his whole body is marked by the narrow lines of the waves, the sea knows him and he knows the sea.

Simão slept. The old man was worried by how quickly sleep overcame him. He remembered how young Simão was: it took an old man like him a lifetime to shut his eyes. Half a century. Alone now, surrounded by sea, he began another journey, a journey into his memory, as dry and barren as the Beloi plain with its spiny jujube trees. He remembered his son, who, on the priest's advice, had decided to leave the island and go to school in Maliana. And how his wife, almost crazed with grief, had taken a mat and a clay pot up to the top of Manukoko and kept a fire burning day and night, awaiting her son's return. And how he, feeling guilty for having taken her son away from her and sent him to a far-off land, like

someone stripping bits of flesh from his own body, had
bought a boat and to punish himself started to sail
around and around the island until reason or the spirits
lit a fire in the middle of the sea to tell him it was time to
go back to his wife's side. He remembered reaching the
top of Manukoko and finding the fire burned out and
his wife's body half devoured by birds. He had given up
the sea then, but, one day, he was told that he would
have to cross the ocean to Díli to fetch his son, who was
coming home. He remembered how his son had said not
a single word to him during the whole crossing. Now, he
relived his son's return (there he was, over there, sleeping); the steersman had spoken to him and had taught
him things about the sea and about the crossing.

After his long absence, his son had been struck dumb.
They gave him the position of chief of the *suku* as a way
of forcing him to speak. They did not understand that he
had left behind him all the tricks in which men wrap
their intentions. He wanted to invent a new language
without those traps and obstacles. The old man only
realized this later, when he began sailing at night and
was the only one awake. He read the language of the
stars, of colours and of the sea. And now his son was
right there in front of him, talking. They understood
each other's words, pauses and silences.

The African slept on, lulled more by the palm wine
than by the sea. He slept the way a child sleeps, with no

thought as to how it's done. He slept like one in full possession of the act of sleeping.

The old man wondered why his island had been chosen as the place to send those whom others punished and did not want. He wondered if the land – which he had loved and where, on a mat, he had loved his wife whom he had later shared with the birds, and where they had engendered a son now cloistered in silence – could become the punishment by fire of which the priest spoke in church. How could he live and survive on a corner of the earth to which others were sent to die? But they slept as calmly as the sea now did. Simão, who still had plenty of time ahead of him, the African with a little time in which to lose himself, and my family continuing their long journey.

In the distance, white strips of light were breaking through the black shadows. Simão woke up. It was a unique moment for someone like him going towards his death; he should hold his breath while contemplating it, as if faced with his own birth.

First, he heard a low rumbling in the depths of the sea. He expected sea horses to appear, like the wild horses near where he lived in Fohorém that used to gallop about, manes flying. Then the troubled waters stirred, grew thick, boiled over. He saw a cone shape open up in the sea and the waters move back to form rigid walls. A ball of fire began to whirl upwards, spinning golden threads about itself. The waves curled and crinkled at the mouth of the cone, drawing up the shining head that was struggling to come to the surface. The sky strained, its face furrowed like the suffering face of a woman at the moment of birth. Then, finally, on the horizon, on a blue platter, a golden *belak** offered itself to the travellers in exchange for the silent bride, for the night that had accompanied them on the crossing.

'There it is!'

He murmured the same words as when, in his own land, he had climbed Mount Tatamailau to see the sun being born. Now they were very close to the island. The bare, black rocks clinging to the back of the cliff which plunged down into the sea blazed in the morning light. The turtle shell grew massive. Immediately ahead of him, the sea beat furiously against the rocks, cursing the old carcass that dared to place itself in its path. The island itself was an intruder, in the heart of the sea. Simão looked at the dry land, where a few clumps of grass still grew. The trees, blackened by the most recent burning, reminded him of the widows who come there to demand that the sea restore their husbands to them, and of the bodies of prisoners who, tortured by longing to return to their own lands, had preferred to perish in that fire so that those across the sea might smell their burned flesh.

---

* A silver or gold circular ornament, worn on the chest.

Seagulls fluttered over the mast, hanging in the air, forgetting where they were going, as if they had momentarily lost the ability to fly. The sea creatures who had kept the boat company throughout the night turned and moved off in an undulating line along the coast.

Simão wanted to put his feet in the water. He looked at the old man, as if seeking his approval. The old man told him that, first, he must wash his hands and then his eyes. Simão had already heard about sharks from his friend Lamartinho, with whom he had studied in Maliana, and who had told him that they were the transmuted forms of his ancestors. No one from the island was ever lost. Sometimes they lived in the sea, sometimes on the land. These cycles demanded their due if they were to continue. Simão had not broken the laws of the ancestors. The offence for which he was being exiled had nothing to do with disrespect for ancient beliefs. The beating he had given the local administrative chief, who had publicly insulted him with actions offending the dignity of his fiancée, merely revealed a desire to hold himself sacred. For each of us is also one of the ancestors. And that in itself was a value to be preserved, however high the price.

'Wash,' the old man said.

Simão cupped his hands and made to scoop up some water. As he leaned over, he saw a shape in the blue depths, as long and white as a scimitar. Hands poised

109,983

above the water, he stared at the shark coming in his direction. He remained absolutely still. The shark stopped inches from the surface. They looked at each other hard, like two passers-by trying to remember where they had seen each other before, flipping quickly through their respective memories. Then the shark performed a pirouette, as if to show itself off, and swam away. Before disappearing completely, it turned one last time to study Simão's attitude and expression. Simão sat as rigid and impassive as a statue.

'He wanted to meet you.' Simão stirred. It was the old man's voice. 'You've just received your first visit from my ancestor. A courtesy call if you like.'

Simão lowered his hands again and scooped up some water. He washed his hands and then splashed his eyes. The steersman skilfully guided the boat through the coral reef separating the rough sea from the quiet waters bathing the beaches of Maumeta. A house with white-washed walls and grass roof, built close to the beach, offered itself to the sea. The walls were coated with salt, and when the tide was high, it must have licked those walls with a lover's fury. Who had had the idea of building a house in this place of story-book romance? What adventurer had decided to up sticks and build a house here of all places, on the very island where Simão had been exiled in order to be eaten away by sadness? An old *gondoeiro* tree with its long beard stood like a faithful sentinel outside this house almost destroyed by storms. The tall tamarind trees reached up into the sky to escape the destructive winds that tore the leaves from the coconut palms and scattered their fruits all along the beach like severed heads in the wake of some wrathful executioner.

When the boat slipped into the shallows, the African woke up. He got to his feet and asked if this was the place he had been sent to; for although he was there to act as prison guard, he knew that he was also an exile. They got out of the boat, stood by the hull and pushed the boat up onto the beach.

'Is this the prisoner?' the corporal meeting the boat asked the steersman, pointing at the African, who had momentarily lost the aplomb lent him by his authority. There were stories of rebellions amongst Africans in the very places where they had been sent to pacify the local rebels. The authorities had witnessed enough fratricidal wars among rival tribes to know that, when trained for the purpose, one native could be used to guard another, and they had no qualms about deploying the survivors of such wars, even if their records were blacker than their skins. And thus they gradually got rid of them as well.

The steersman averted his gaze to avoid a question which he had failed to answer throughout the crossing. It would be like acknowledging himself to be a jailer. Simão did not speak either; it was not for him to reply.

During the silence of the crossing, he had promised himself that a new era was about to begin. In that place of death and oblivion, he promised himself a new life.

The African recovered his composure, felt in his back pocket for the prisoner's papers and handed them to his superior. Simão picked up his suitcase and followed the others in military file. First the corporal, then the African and then him. He felt freer having no one behind him to watch his steps. He turned round and murmured, 'Apart from . . .'

Simão broke off abruptly as he caught sight of an imposing, indolent figure emerging like a ghost from the white house near the wave-battered stone quay. It was as if he were looking at himself. Simão had been about to say 'Apart from the sea', but the sea, at that moment, was in the eyes of Mário Lopes, blazing forth from that prominent brow, from that broad face with its fleshy lips and gleaming bald pate sprinkled with a few tightly curled white hairs. He wore trousers and a loose white shirt disguising a large, tremulous belly; he was supported by two long bow-legs that trembled beneath him when he left his house to manage his shop in the town of Maumeta.

He was a *malae-metam*, an African, and a wealthy exile, originally from São Tomé e Príncipe. He had acquired a coaster (*corocora*), in which he transported dried fish to Díli, returning with provisions, clothes, beer, Coca-Cola and other merchandise which he would sometimes lay out on the beach when he disembarked, revealing contraband tobacco that made you dizzy when you smoked it, and melted chocolates that provoked intestinal rumblings and diarrhoea. It was also rumoured that he smuggled books and subversive ideas which he then preached at birthday parties, baptisms, weddings and especially funerals, imitating the catechism teacher's funeral rhetoric to create real masterpieces of denunciation, rehabilitating the memory of the deceased prisoner and placing the blame fairly and squarely on the authorities for those banished by death or exile. He was said to have excellent handwriting and a sharp pen, and some on the island used his services. He had a rival, one Senhor Queiroz – known as the *ain aat*, the lame, white foreigner – in carrying out these intimidatory tasks: together they terrorized the administrative authorities and the local rulers, who stole other people's women and goods. Anyone who had received unfair treatment went to them for help in petitioning the governor for reparation.

We were given a large house with bamboo walls and a grass roof where snakes nested and from which they performed lightning sorties in pursuit of the rats that sometimes sought shelter beneath my sleeping-mat, leaving their marks on my skin. My mother was superstitious and feared that the wounds were, in fact, left by the claws of Pontiana, the spirit of seduction. So at night, she would mount guard at my bedside, light a candle and say the rosary, and, as if that were not enough, she would resort to the use of a long, sharp nail and a lime.

She would wait until midnight, the hour when the grey dove sings and the time, my mother believed, when that bird of the night is transformed into the lady of death. When nothing happened, she would snuff out the candle, put away her rosary, and leave me clutching the nail in one hand and the lime in the other, with the task of hunting down a Pontiana-turned-rat.

It was a large house with many rooms, as though the builder had guessed that nurses were bound to have a lot of children, few of whom would die at birth. Even so, some of the rooms remained empty and dark; no one went into them and my mother imagined she could hear noises, the voices and laments of dead relatives, who took advantage of their state to demand favours and tributes. She used the priest's monthly visit to fill those rooms with people preparing for baptism, people from Maquili, Macadade, Beloi and Biqueli, whose presence, she believed, would drive out those souls in torment.

The chief of the local administration was safely ensconced at the top of the road that led up from the sea in a palace encircled by a high whitewashed stone wall to protect him and his family and his mango trees, whose perfumed fruits attracted bats and owls from every corner of the island, providing a shrill soundtrack to the night. (Since there was no prison for him, Simão was appointed watchman for this orchard, and so came to live in the same house as the authorities themselves.) As there was talk of secret landings by Indonesians disguised as fishermen, the administration also protected its grounds with African exiles, island residents and a group of hunters whose quarters were surrounded by barbed wire. It was an island besieged by small fears.

The diocese of Díli had sent two teachers to teach the catechism and primary school subjects.

One was from Laclubar and had studied at the Catholic mission of Soibada. He had married the daughter of one of the local rulers of Suro and adopted an aristocratic pose, austere and severe. His credentials were his own adolescent sons who were studying at the seminary in Dare and who, one stormy day, had ventured across the sea in a boat with a few other colleagues and teachers; when they finally reached the town, they collapsed, on the beach, horribly seasick, but at least safe from becoming a sumptuous meal for the sharks. They wore modest shorts (which covered their modest knees) and the eternal smile of adolescents illuminated by grace; when they went to church to sing the *Te Deum* and other Gregorian chants, they stood with heads bowed and eyes mystically glazed. They were my first contact with the young men who lived in the gleaming tin-roofed edifice in Dare, which stood like an eagle's nest perched high above the city of Díli.

The other teacher was a strong, rustic fellow. He had been given the task of setting up a catechism school in

Biqueli – near the hot springs that were the refuge of 'peelers' or people who suffered from skin diseases – a rival to Dona Juliana who had established a Protestant church there and who exchanged correspondence and general good neighbourliness with her fellow believers on the Indonesian island of Lira. So he was the front line of the Catholic church, and watched his opponent's every move. I was taught that Protestants were *taca-matam* – they closed their eyes when they said their prayers. During mass and prayers at the Catholic church in Maumeta, I was chosen as a guard or defender of the faith, scrutinizing the faces of the faithful and those preparing for baptism for any drooping eyelids that would reveal them as interlopers. I found, however, that during prayers and long litanies everyone fell asleep, and that during mass everyone closed their eyes to meditate or out of sheer exhaustion.

The school on Ataúro was a large house full of desks, and the floor was covered with a long mat, which when there were earth tremors reminded me of a flying carpet. My father bought me a slate and a slate pencil and hoped that I never lacked for saliva.

First, I was taught the catechism in Tetum, then the national anthem in Portuguese and, finally, a few hymns in Latin. Later I was taught to write the alphabet, numbers and the times tables. Then there were the words we learned in our reader, r-o-*ro*-l-a-*la* (*rola*, pigeon), which

I knew meant what I called *lakateu* in Tetum, because that was what the picture showed. It was the *lakateu* that I kept in my head, and in my pocket, captured after painful pursuits during the rainy season, when, its wings wet and weary, it would finally surrender easily. G-a-*ga-l-o-lo* (*galo*, cockerel) was *manu-aman* because there was a picture of a *manu-aman*, though it lacked the brilliant colours of the Sunday market cockfights. And it was on Sundays that Simão would climb the white wall with a fighting cock under each arm. People said that in the silence of the administrator's palace he bred cockerels that were fierce and tenacious fighters, that he sharpened their spurs and experimented with deadly poisons. However, this reputation was derived more from the fact that he was an exile from Loro Monu*, an area rich in enigmas and magic spells cast in the secrecy of the frontier regions. He encouraged it, dyeing his fighters odd colours to conceal their natural plumage from the owners of opposing cockerels, who believed they could judge the fierceness of a bird from the colour combinations of its feathers. His reputation rested, above all, on his ability to disguise the *sikat*, some abnormality of colour or plumage, the magic feather that is said to mark a cockerel out as a winner.

Although in the Drawing and Composition classes the

---

* An expression meaning 'where the sun sets', used to describe the western half of East Timor.

subjects were mainly domestic animals, these were gradually replaced by the pear and the apple and other distant, paradisiacal fruits that made our mouths water, but which we only knew from our readers and occasional Biblical references. Compositions were always written in praise of our distant motherland, symbolized and guarded by two male angels far uglier than those in any sacred images, and whose portraits hung on the wall facing us. One was bald and fat and wore white decorated with gold lace. The other was gloomy and serious, dressed in a grey suit and possessed of a sharp, threatening nose and hair combed smooth in the style of the soldiers and the *cipaios*. I was told that these angels were represented in Timor by the pale-skinned blond sergeant, the commander of the barracks, whom I feared because of his resemblance to the *rain-nain*, the spirit of the earth, confirming my mother's belief that white men had erupted in flames out of the earth's centre. And my fear intensified whenever I saw him, rifle in hand, in pursuit of the grey and green doves which sought refuge on the island from the burnings that devastated the other islands every year, surrounding us in a ring of fire.

From time to time a twin-engined plane would roar in. It brought important people – missionaries and inspectors – and galvanized my father into enlisting the entire family to sort out the infirmary, which with its rotten beams and supports was on the verge of collapse.

GALWAY COUNTY LIBRARIES

He feared for the orange tree that grew near the house and produced sweet, juicy fruit, and was said to have been brought there and tended by a traveller from the island of Kisar. Everyone knew the fruit had some medicinal value but only later did they tell me that they were manly fruits, for they gave strength to men brought low by women. Indeed, there were rumours of all sorts of good and secret things to be found on the surrounding islands, such as fruit trees, spells and dazzlingly beautiful women.

The missionaries would baptize the catechumens with the names of kings and prophets. They inaugurated whole native dynasties of Afonso Henriques and Vasco da Gamas, or of such muscular prophets as Samson and Moses.

3

He always arrived when the kerosene lamp was being lit. He was a soldier, a Firaku, from the region near Mount Matebian in easternmost Timor, who liked to strike commanding poses. He plied my cousin Rosa, who took care of me, with sweets. He ended up having to take care of me too, but after pressing a sweet into my hand would simply tell me to get lost. He held my cousin's hand and they would stroll along the beach. They oohed and aahed whenever they spotted some errant car churning up dust along the distant road that ran beside Areia Branca beach near Díli. He used to tell stories from the Bible in the same sing-song voice with which he named the soldiers in his troop: Adam and Eve, Joseph and his brothers, Moses and his tablets, Samson and his hair. I learned all the plots by heart, and sometimes they frightened me and sometimes they drew tears from my family, who were touched by these foreign stories that gripped young and old alike.

One day, I was charged with carrying a secret message from my enamoured cousin to the tent surrounded by barbed wire where this local centurion lived. I saw his

Bible, hidden on his bedside table along with various others – the military rule book, a manual on mines and traps, and photographs of white, naked women whom I supposed to be angels walking in the garden of Eden before the fall of Adam. The Bible was a fat, heavy book that smelled old and musty. There was Eve, naked, covering her breasts and her post-virginity. Adam was gloomily trying to conceal his sin before the smiling snake coiled about the apple tree, while the angel Gabriel angrily pointed to the road into exile. There was the enraged prophet Moses, blowing smoke from his nostrils, with the tablets and the ten commandments, ready to hurl them down onto the heads of his pursuers, who were doubtless sinners too.

The love affair ended and the soldier disappeared. My cousin was left like a faded rose, and my furious father cut off all her hair. My mother took pity on her, though, and sent her back to Manufahi. I inherited the book and the stories, which I continued to tell. Stories to make people weep and that blamed the ancestors for their children's current misfortunes. Stories that are still lived out today.

Mário Lopes wanted to revive his business and so he sent to Díli for a baker and former soldier from the Beiras region of Portugal, who on arrival immediately set to felling the gum trees. His destruction was equal to the natives' slash-and-burn techniques. The man was called

Eanes, and, once his military service in East Timor was over, he had married a local woman. Until he came, neither I nor my schoolmates who had been born on the island had ever eaten bread. It was the food of the Portuguese. All we had was the tasteless wafer proffered during communion. We wanted men's bread, round and spongy, but they gave us God's bread instead, thin stuff that you were forbidden even to chew. Now Vasco, the son of Mário Lopes the exile, started turning up every morning smelling of freshly baked bread, his mouth smeared with butter. During break, he would unwrap a rose-patterned handkerchief containing bread and butter which would make us all drool and feel even angrier that we too were not the sons of proper exiles. One day, the miracle happened. He promised bread and butter as a reward for anyone who would write his composition for him. And so, stealing stories from the Bible, by the light of the kerosene lamp and accompanied by my usual night visitors, I began earning my daily bread. I found out later that it had been Mário Lopes' idea to encourage my taste for writing, chuckling subversively at my childish imagination.

At the end of the school year, my father took me to Mário Lopes' shop. I was expecting a prize for passing and lingered by the toy cabinet full of motorcycles, planes and cars. I decided I would choose a Harley-Davidson. (Years later, in Lisbon, when I decided to try out a real motorbike of the same make, the black gloves I was given to wear bore the label 'Made in Indonesia'.) Despite all my pleas and supplications, my stubborn father asked for a green suitcase made of tin. Then he said to Dona Aquilina, 'Fill it with three pairs of blue shorts, three white shirts, a pair of white pumps and a pair of white socks. Oh, and don't forget the beret, please. In blue!'

While I looked on, overwhelmed by such extravance and such whiteness, he added, still in blue mode, 'And two sizes too large!'

Dona Aquilina opened her eyes wide in astonishment, and I assumed that these were clothes intended for my brother, so that he could join the Portuguese Youth. The lady felt my bony, protuberant ribs and pulled a face. She went to stroke my hair, but my father stopped her, believing that, in order to prepare myself for the times ahead, I should never expect anyone's pity.

'He'll grow! And until he does, he can pad himself out with kapok!' he concluded abruptly.

So it was that I left my parents on the island of Ataúro and returned across the sea to Díli. It was a stormy day and I appreciated my father's farsightedness in choosing kapok as a complement to my wardrobe. Had he chosen lead from Macadade, I would have gone straight to the bottom.

Simão eventually married Ermelinda and went to live

in the *suku* of Macadade, where he became the local chief. Lamartinho remained dumb, but married Esmeralda, who spoke for herself, for him and for both of them. I cried throughout the entire crossing, and the old steersman respected my distress and said nothing. I realized later that this silence was his way of showing solidarity with his own son. When we reached Lecidere beach and he handed me over to the relatives who had come from Manufahi, charged with taking me to Same before my imprisonment in the school at Soibada, the old man placed in my hands some dry dust, the same colour as his eyes, which, like the island of Ataúro, were forbidden to shed tears or rain. He said to me, 'Be sure to come back! After all, you've got arms and legs to swim with.'

4

My Uncle Armindo was waiting for me with a diminutive horse, just my size. We rode up narrow paths to the town of Aileu and then to chilly Maubisse from where we could see Mount Cabalaqui. In Same my grandparents were waiting for me; they had never left, apart from during the war of Manufahi, when they had taken shelter amidst the peaks of Leolaku. After the defeat, in order to survive the victors' predations, they hid amongst the coffee plantations and the sea of cacao, amongst the damp and the mist, amongst the smell of tobacco and *laku** and in the shadows of their own ghosts.

Manufahi was the spiritual source of my ancestors that I needed to plumb before entering the Catholic mission of Soibada. My grandfather Manucoli, the old *assuwain* or warrior, introduced me to relatives and to sacred places, mysteries and spells. He wanted me to know my own nature before seeing it forever submerged in the Christian world. He would wake me in the

---

* The palm civet, a small marsupial commonly found in coffee plantations. The musk from its anal glands is used in perfumery.

morning when he was about to go to the spring, always carrying eggs he had gathered the previous night to give as an offering to the eel that lived in the spring and protected the source, keeping the aquifers clean. Years later, a foolhardy relative of mine was paralysed down his left side for daring to kill an eel, thus blocking the flow of water and drying up the spring. My grandfather showed me the *surik* or sword that he had used in time of war and I saw that there were still bloodstains on it from a time preserved in the layers of moss and lichen on its petrified face. It looked as if it had been hewn out of the rocks on the mountains, green and ancient.

I was introduced to the teacher, Mário de Noronha, who had married the only daughter of the *liurai* Dom Boaventura and whose children went to the school at Soibada, children with whom I would share both journey and prison. Mário de Noronha was a catechism teacher, and, as such, a safeguard for the daughter of the rebellious leader and for her other relatives and followers. He was the *ai-hum* – the protective tree – for the defeated of Manufahi. I felt reassured by the fact that he would be sponsoring my entry into that school which had come to be seen as a privileged place for teachers and taught alike, patriots loyal to the Portuguese flag. But that commitment cost me dear: when anyone asked me where I came from and I started dividing myself up amongst the various places I had lived, someone would answer for me

that I was from Manufahi, immediately dubbing me a
rebel however loudly I protested that I was from Ataúro
and however hard I tried to prove this by my swimming
prowess, for I could swim as well as any Ataúro shark. I
was in no way a rebel. I was seven years old and very
timid and thin. I was thrust into the little band of *lusitos*,
separated from any relatives or friends amongst the
younger boys (*infantes*), and from protectors amongst
the older boys (*vanguardistas*), none of whom could possibly help me, since they were forbidden to speak to
anyone outside these respective *castelos* into which the
Portuguese Youth Movement had divided them.

The school was named after Dom Nuno Álvares
Pereira. It was a bastion of Portugal in the very heart of
Timor, a reminder of the hero of that far-off battle of
Aljubarrota, when the Portuguese defeated the Spanish.
This would be the arena for the fencing and fighting
bouts that I would have to win, as my father had done
before me. Any hint of old, pagan values was completely
forbidden. Stories were told of pupils who had run away
from the mission several times only to be sent back by
their parents; the native circle was tightening, purging
itself of contaminated elements in order to keep the
tribal system strong and alive.

The mission was a group of tin-roofed buildings made
out of stone and red clay. It was a real Tower of Babel
where boys from all over Timor converged, speaking

many different languages. Then there were the teachers. Egídio, the skinny one, who always wore a scarf around his neck and moved softly and elegantly like a strange bird. He taught music to the third years. He had the tormented face of a Beethoven who had taken refuge in this tropical forest in order to compose diluvian operas. In Soibada it rained all year round. He chose me to join the choir, which sang long Latin songs during the seemingly endless night-time masses, accompanied by the loud snores of the *vanguardista* loafers lulled to sleep by monotonous sermons. On my way to the school, I had been warned about Master Jaime, who supervised the students and whose reputation as a tyrant had spread throughout the area and become a kind of aura he encouraged. He was darker than his own shadow, and the merest whiff of his presence made me pee in my pants from fear. He rode a white horse and, with his whip in his hand, looked like a copy of some portrait of Napoleon, forcing the boarders to go for long treks through muddy, rainy landscapes in search of wood and stone to rebuild the school walls, and making the captains of the various *castelos* whip their underlings as they slowly weeded the garden. He was a Pharaonic figure. Fortunately, Egídio was my teacher. Next door to us, Master Jaime turned his classroom into a torture chamber. We would close our ears to the cries, laments and insults coming through the wall. He denounced his students for being as stupid as *kuda-burros*, not that anyone knew what that was. Being a *kuda* (horse), it certainly had four legs, but the rebellious student could only guess at the meaning of *burro* or 'donkey'. Only much later did I actually see an example of this beast in a market in Lisbon. It bore no resemblance to the students at Soibada or even to Master Jaime. He used to clean the blackboard with his pupils' dark faces; according to him, having their faces covered in white chalk dust brought them a little enlightenment. He forced the most stubborn amongst them to crawl about beneath the desks, ordering the others to kick them as a way of teaching them a lesson.

Dressed in the regulation brown trousers and green shirt, Master Jaime was in charge of the Portuguese Youth. On parade days, he would order them to play the cornet and drum and to march up and down before the crowds, saluting those in authority, both present and absent. He was the gym master too, and so luckless members of the Portuguese Youth would also have to lie on the ground, wearing baggy shorts – it wasn't yet the season for long johns – opening and closing their legs before the cruel laughter of the populace and the averted faces of the blushing female visitors who had come from the local Canossian school for the festivities. At his most inspired, he would declare that he only wanted the best for us, in his own way, that knowledge had a price, and it was up to him to set that price. That long, thin streak of a man carried out his mission rigorously. He was setting his mark on race-horses.

Then there was Fernando Osório Soares. When I first saw him at the mission, mingling with the other teachers, who, at the time, were required to wear Western clothes, I thought he was the chief of some *suku*, who had gone there to ask for money or to demand recompense. He was tall, white-haired, very erect, with large, muddy, bare feet. He wore a green-check sarong and a brown khaki shirt. I could hardly believe it when he was introduced as the teacher of the second years: he looked like a native, full of an ancestral, pagan wisdom that seemed incompatible with the teaching of Portuguese grammar, reading and multiplication tables. At most, he looked like a teacher of catechism in Tetum. (The official directive that public servants should dress like Westerners, as befitted their position, extended this 'prerogative' to their families. My mother had already expressed her disgust at this when, one day, my father returned home bearing his monthly wages and informed her that his bosses had told him that the wives of public servants should replace their traditional dress with Western clothes. She replied that there comes a time in one's life when change can only mean catastrophe and that she had no intention of looking ridiculous, wearing Western-style dress whilst chewing betel like a native.)

Master Fernando exuded serenity. At the time, my head was filled with terrifying tales about thieves who, it was said, used to steal children and boil them down to feed the machines that made money, and I always slept best when it was Master Fernando's turn to stand guard over the dormitory. He had a son who was studying for the priesthood, but was utterly unperturbed when that son failed to become a priest. He took pride in his own work, and did not need his family to increase his own prestige.

Then there was Master Alberto, who now lives in Lisbon. He was from the Lacló region, the kingdom loyal to the Portuguese authorities, and although he was always inciting the students to beat each other up, he himself never did so. He seemed like a character out of a travelling circus. He cured the bites of rats, scorpions and snakes, using suggestion only, and would drive out malaria by unleashing a yell that terrified the patient back into health.

Master Narciso Lobato would occasionally go off hunting, returning at dawn during morning mass with red deer and roe deer slung over his horses, which made me dream of some improvement in our diet – perhaps a little rice and meat. The daily ration of maize gave me continual stomach-ache; it came mixed with a few careless rats and the sweat from the brow of the overworked cook, Balthazar, my father's godson. Thanks to this baptismal relationship, and given my rachitic state, my diet was supplemented with a little roast cassava that he slipped under the lid of my desk each day. But I was not as lucky as some of my classmates, who were sent into the orchard to pick its delicious fruit, although they were known for ever after as *koko*, or 'tasters', because they competed with the *laku* and the mice, with the owls and other birds in testing the ripeness of the fruit.

From time to time, we would be visited by someone in a position of authority. When it was the governor, the festive spirit took over and the school was decked out with arches made from bamboo and palm leaves. The school song would be sung and the fourth-year students would give thunderous renditions of cantos from the great Portuguese epic *The Lusiads*, which they would occasionally forget, as if on purpose, guaranteeing Master Jaime even more praise for prompting them and astounding the visiting dignitary that one man could both possess and be able to impart so much knowledge. Although the school had been built in the midst of those hills, like an altar to learning, with people from different races and speaking different languages, Portuguese was compulsory in the grounds, and anyone who disobeyed would receive a sharp rap with a ruler. The cane or the ruler proved harsh but effective. During the day, the cane would be passed from one change of the linguistic guard to the next, who would sometimes lay traps in order to obtain the evidence they needed more quickly.

By the end of the year, I was left with only one set of
cloths that clung to my skin and stank to high heaven.
My relatives from Manufahi who were supposed to
come and collect me failed to turn up. All the other students had left for home. So those of us from Ataúro
decided to walk across the fields of Samoro as far as
Laclubar in search of help. We got a lift in an old army
truck to Díli. In the very place where I had once waited
with my family, another steersman informed me that my
parents had been transferred to Lautém, in the easternmost part of Timor. I embraced my classmates and said
goodbye, though I longed to go with them to Ataúro,
where I had seen the sun rise for the first time as if for
me alone. I was told that the old steersman had gone
away. He had set out to sea in a small boat when he realized from his swollen, flaking skin that death was near. I
was told that Lamartinho had recovered his speech and
that Esmeralda was expecting a baby, and that Simão
had gone off to be a soldier in Macadade.

It took a whole day to travel the coast road to Lautém
in a Chinese bus, fitted with planks for the passengers,
and home, too, to some very pampered fleas, grown fat
on many journeys and on many succulent victims. The
north coast is very arid, with just a sprinkling of acacias,
white gum trees and tamarinds. A few deep river valleys
cut across the vast plains, and these were planted with
ricefields bounded by casuarina trees that sang and

danced in the wind. After Metinaro, Manatuto, Laleia, Vemassi, Baucau, Laga and Laivai, Lautém appeared before us like a pale lady who, in the grip of madness, had been abandoned by her husband. Beside the sea, bearing the brunt of the violent weather, stood the erect but crumbling walls of ruined, white, colonial-style houses, the interiors overgrown with weeds. I was afraid that this was where my parents were now living. The bus did not stop, however, despite the white sign announcing that this was the town of Lautém. Instead it accelerated as if the driver had seen a ghost, and the dust along the dirt road enveloped in a white cloud that remnant of what had once been a brilliant, seaside town. The real Lautém had been moved inland to a pleasant location near a lake rich in shrimp and surrounded by ancient trees that sheltered monkeys by day and owls by night.

Lautém terrified intruders. It was a land of proud, passionate men, all speakers of Fataluko. They guarded their honour with swords, which they always carried with them and were quick to use. Very few *calades*, *bunaks* or *macassaes* dared leave their lands to marry a *dagadá* woman*, for they were said to be astonishingly beautiful, and no one then could possibly afford the head of cattle or bride-price necessary to support such a

---

* *Calades* are an ethnological group living in East Timor, mainly speaking Mambae. *Bunaks* come from the Bobonaro region, *macassaes* from Baucau and the *dagadá* from Lospalos.

union. There were tales too of vendettas dating back
hundreds of years, like the revenge carried out by a
woman who arrived at the administrator's house bearing
her husband's head, saying that she had cut it off to
repay an ancient debt, for an ancestor of hers who had
been killed by the family of her now decapitated husband. In Lautém boats came ashore from the
neighbouring Indonesian islands to trade at the bazaar.
They brought goats, pigs, sheep, cockerels, sweetmeats
made from palm hearts, and oranges – lovely, juicy
oranges from Kisar. In exchange they took back with
them sarongs, lengths of cloth and trinkets that cost the
local traders nothing.

Lautém was a very long way from Soibada and, following my experiences there, I arrived at my parents'
new home showing symptoms of tuberculosis, which
saved me from ever having to go back to the school in
Soibada. The military had built a primary school in
Lautém, but there was no one to teach the fourth years,
the nine-year-olds. Every Thursday, an Italian priest
came to celebrate mass in Fataluko; he was a colossus of
a man who used to squeeze his gladiatorial bulk onto a
tiny red Lambretta. My father discussed with him the
possibility of my being accepted at the Salesian school
that had been set up on the edge of the vast plateau of
Fuiloro where you could still see the mounds of earth
into which the Japanese had stuck pointed stakes to stop

Australian planes from landing during the Second World War.

So, perched on the back of Father Júlio's scooter, I arrived at the mission. Whereas in Soibada the mountainous terrain demanded ancient methods of cultivation for its uneven, stony fields, involving the missionary in repeated blessings of apparently sterile seeds, in Fuiloro the Salesians went in for intensive farming, using various types of modern machinery. Boarders were only used as labour when it was deemed absolutely necessary or of some educational value, though without its ever being oppressive. The rigour and weight of the Portuguese Youth Movement was similarly absent. Although lessons at the school were given in Portuguese, there were also missionaries from Spain and Italy. The church brought together what various treaties had tried to keep apart. My teacher in the fourth year was a Portuguese lay brother, whose medium build and white skin told me he was from the province of Minho. And I would gaze up at the ceiling, trying to conjure that Imperial North out of the tangle of spiders' webs. He tried to show us a different side of life in Portugal, relaxed, folkloric and fun, with no heroes or martyrs. Every week, he would bring his gramophone along and interrupt our studies with records of classical music and the poetry of Fernando Pessoa read by João Villaret, inspiring me to declaim poems too, imitating his warm, full voice: O *menino da sua mãe*, 'His mother's little boy'. And there were the inevitable *fados* and traditional dance tunes, followed, naturally enough, by songs from the Eurovision song contest. But most wonderful of all was *Non ho l'età* sung by a young Italian woman, whom I imagined to be as beautiful as Our Lady, and who broke our hearts with her sweet voice. And Father Júlio agreed: *Non ho l'età* – 'I'm too young for love!'

Although I knew that I would never visit the Portugal shown to me in the tourist guides – our schoolbooks – I delighted in imagining its cities, mountains, rivers, its people and language. I loved knowing of the existence, the possibility, of earthly paradises and promised lands, perhaps especially since there was no chance of such a thing in my own life. It was in my fourth year that I discovered the route taken by the discoverers back to Portugal. Macau and its capital, the City of the Holy Name of God. Goa, Daman and Diu; lost, lamented India. Mozambique as long and thin as the giraffe in Gorongosa Park. Angola grown fat on the diamonds of North and South Lunda and the oil of Cabinda. The São Tomé e Príncipe Islands of Mário Lopes and cacao. Guinea-Bissau and the Bijagós archipelago. Cape Verde and the mournful music of Mindelo. Madeira and the Azores. Brazil and Dom Pedro's historic cry of 'Independence or death!'. Portugal and Entroncamento, the railway junction where all the world's trains met. Sometimes, remembering my mother's suspicions, I doubted the existence of these lands. But sheer delight made me believe in those distant places as I did in the paradise lost by Adam and gained by death. I should have believed too in earthly paradises that were nearer to hand and more real.

When I finished my fourth year, my father could already speak Fataluko well and had grown fond of the region. He asked to stay on there. I was destined for Díli, where I would join my other brothers who had gone on to secondary school there, but had left before the end. That gave my father divine aspirations: he felt it was time we had a priest in the family. He spoke to the head of the school, who had serious doubts about me. He said that I was too fond of life to be of any use to God. Nevertheless, he allowed me to be selected for the seminary, first urging on me reflection and much penitence as a most redeeming experience.

5

When I went down to Díli – you always go down to the city, even if you approach it by sea – I was often told not to forget where I was from. But I felt I was from several places. Whenever anyone asked, I always said Ataúro. Only later was I told that your home is where you were born. So I should have said Cailaco. When I went to get my identity card, even before I was asked, I had already announced that I was from Cailaco, immediately adding 'in the municipality of Bobonaro', and, as if to plead some extenuating circumstance for that remote region, that hiding place and altar of rebels, I supplemented this with, 'Province of Timor!'

'Ah, Bobonaro! The land of *kuda-uluns*!' said the mulatto functionary in an ironic tone. His skin was blotchy with vitiligo.

He grabbed my index finger with all his strength, as if intent on breaking it, and pressed it down hard on a pad of black ink and then on a piece of card, leaving a dark smudge which I imagined to be a reflection of my skin or a photograph of my pagan soul. I had done my best to give an acceptable sequence to the facts, emphasizing the final phrase in which I deposited all the patriotism I had been filled with at school. Despite this, I was sent straight back to the most purely native part of my origins.

'You lot don't fool anyone!' He paused, taking careful aim. 'You eat what you ride!' quipped this philosophical clerk.

He looked at my photograph, from which my frightened eyes shone like a *laku*'s, and tugged my ear, indicating to me the way out. I left with his promise that I would not have to wait long, just long enough for the moon to enter a new phase and for the snakes to shed their skin, for me to change my legal status. After that, armed with my identity card, I could prove that I was a responsible citizen and would never again be subjected to the mockery of some civil servant, belittling me because I came from the interior and belonged to an ethnic group who had acquired a reputation for dining on horses' heads and for neighing in their sleep and in moments of ecstasy or rage.

'*Kuda-ulum!*' I kept saying as I headed towards the Bebora district, across the tarmac road that burned my bare feet (I had no money for the bus), constantly startled by the tinkling bicycle bells of the Chinese as they wheeled wildly past – a different social class.

Bebora was an outlying district full of *palapa* – houses thatched with palm leaves – near the airfield, where the domestic planes spent the night, and near the field where Arab traders who ate no pork used to stay. Timor was a mosaic of providers of delicacies and renouncers of all things porky. Bebora was on the side of the city where the heat was most intense; the sweat poured off everyone and the dust that rose up in phantasmagorical shapes frightened the herds of pigs rooting around in the alleyways near the houses, disputing leftovers and territory with a few starving, scrawny dogs. Taking refuge in that collection of houses were minor civil servants, stonemasons and carpenters, small businessmen, people with no job, streetsellers and innumerable young men who had finished their primary education in the mission schools in the interior but, having no vocation for the priesthood, had come to Díli to try their luck. They would move in with some reasonably well-off relatives, though always keeping a link with the interior as a source of food and psychological support. The mountains were like an eternal fallback, which had been exchanged for an often fictitious hope that lived like an interloper in the city. The relative I stayed with worked for the post office. He mended wires and telephones and communicated using Morse code. I felt as if I were at the centre of the whole tangle of wires that crisscrossed the island and served to guide travellers. He had provided a home to my brothers, who had since disappeared off into the city.

While I was waiting for my identity card, before going up the hill to Dare, I counted the days off on my rosary beads, the number of days left before my cloistered existence began. For me, Dare was the house with the tin roof that you could see from Ataúro because it reflected the sun's rays like a lighthouse. Dare had come to me in the form of that group of seasick tourists who had crossed the sea to Ataúro one stormy day and, having been spared becoming an addition to the sharks' diet, had gone to the church as soon as they could to praise the Almighty, singing the *Te Deum* as I had never heard it sung.

When people asked me where I was going, I said: the seminary. They would then deliberately lard their conversation with foul language, imitating the soldiers and the military world in general, expecting me instantly to cover my ears with my hands. Since I didn't understand a word they were saying, they eventually gave up and told me instead that there was some very good singing there, that you got to play basketball, and that you studied until your hair turned white and your eyes went blind, but that some students managed to escape to enjoy the delights of the Colmera district. Colmera was situated on the very road I had to travel between Bebora and the Tarmac City of central Dili. I used to pretend to close my eyes when I passed through there alongside the army recruits, living it up with the prostitutes, and the penniless vagrants who hurled insults at them. Many a door was closed in my face when I tried to gain entry to *korem-metam* parties*, the justification being that God had no time for the good life and that I too must renounce worldly pleasures. And so, on Saturday evenings, I would watch my brothers carefully pull on their brightly striped, bell-bottom Terylene trousers, plaster their hair with brilliantine, and then go off to trawl the outlying districts in search of places where some lady of easy virtue would furtively let them into the house. As I fell asleep, I would hear, in the distance, violin solos played by Abril Metam and guitars keeping the steady rhythm of a waltz, or the playfully romantic tones of Brazilian singers like Teixeirinha and Roberto Carlos, as well as sentimental country and western music from America. A medley of sound fit to break your heart. When I insisted on knowing about life – from which I was supposedly excluded by a predestined abstinence – my brothers would try to dissuade me by calling me a failed priest, even before I had become one, as if they could read in my eyes and in the palm of my hand an unfrocked future.

Following the inevitable advice of the parish activists, I was an assiduous attendant of holy mass at Motael church, whose holy exit was even more crowded than

---

* A party held one year after the death of a friend or relative.

the church itself. All week this moment was eagerly awaited by the younger members of the civil service, in possession of a career and qualifications and in search of nicely brought up young ladies to be wooed with the promise of marriage, bed and children. Some even temporarily abandoned the ladies of the *korem-metam*. At night, my relatives and I would gather round the radio to listen to the passionate words of love, scorn or menace, wrapped up, of course, in the music of Teixeirinha and Roberto Carlos, and addressed to a certain princess who lived in Ai-Lele Hum or to the fool who had dared to get in the way of the lone horseman who loved her. When the programme finished, the lights were switched off and Díli sank into silence, apart from the barking of dogs in the distance. It was time to make way for the ghosts, drunks and lunatic pursuers of Pontiana, the spirit of seduction.

Sunday afternoons were devoted to football. There were teams from Díli – offshoots of Portuguese teams like Benfica, Sporting and Académica – regional teams like Aileu and Café, and the local União with their players and managers straight out of the missionary schools. The stadium was next to the market place which offered another attraction to the men from the outlying districts: cockfighting and the attendant betting, where victories were greeted loud and long with *aclalas* (warcries) that rose up above the shouts of 'Sai-asso' – 'Get off!' – with which the soldiers stationed in Díli greeted the referees. My sympathies were with Académica for whom my brother played, and I would furiously polish his boots as if a better shine guaranteed a better performance. They also had José Alexandre Gusmão, goalkeeper and ex-seminarian, who was too busy making up sonnets to actually stop any goals*. If Académica were defeated I became the butt of the other boys' scorn for having bet on the wrong bird. But the team I really couldn't resist was União, whose fans insulted the referees in Tetum and whose players, still under the influence of the music of Abril Metam, came direct from the *korem-metam*, were sick in the corner of the field and stretchered off before the game was over.

The diocese of Díli was the marshalling point for those going up the hill to Dare. On the appointed day, there we were, accompanied by the relatives who were seeing us off. There were no tears. No one cried because going to the seminary and being placed in the hands of the Jesuits was like going from Purgatory to Heaven. Among our number, I saw the familiar faces of friends from my schools in Soibada and Fuiloro. They had merely grown taller and fatter. Some boys were already in knee-length shorts, and their eyes seemed to reflect the long hours of preparation and reflection they had put in during the

* As Xamana Gusmão, he became the guerrilla leader of the independence movement in Timor.

holidays. They had ordered the seminary emblem and insignia. I felt embarrassed at my own lack of preparation and reflection. We were all crammed into the bus like chicks in a cage. The bus, which usually carried the girls from the school in Canto Resende, was immediately pursued by noisy motorcyclists who only realized their mistake when they were shrouded in Lahane dust as the bus turned off up the dirt road. Three-quarters of an hour later, we were in the middle of a group of yellow buildings surrounded by coffee plantations that were shaded by broad trees – *Albizia mollucana*. It looked like a farm. It was a precursor to the former administrative post at Laulara, where someone had tried to create a botanical garden with plants from all over the Far East. A kind of tropical Sintra. It smelled of sandalwood, cinnamon, durian fruit and coffee.

The school was named after St Francis Xavier and had been a teacher-training college. It received first-year seminary students – ten-year-olds – and selected from them those who had a true vocation for the priesthood. It was run by a Timorese missionary from Letefoho and two teachers from Ermera. Although they were all from the best coffee-planting areas in Timor and the school was rather like a farm, none of them had any talent for agricultural activities, and a certain Master José Maria used to recruit young men from Atsabe to perform these tasks: they formed a rural Catholic militia.

Coming, as we did, straight from indigenous rural life
to a city divided between the tarmac centre occupied by
the Chinese and the native periphery of dirt roads, few of
us would have had much chance of getting into the secondary school or the technical school in Díli. Not that all
of us wanted to be priests. We stayed there until God
decided otherwise or for as long as His representatives
allowed us to. The subjects taught were the same as at
secondary school, with the addition of Choral Singing
and Ethics. In Soibada, Master Egídio had gone to great
lengths to train my voice. Here, though, the staves and
the rhythms of tonic sol-fa did not attract me and I felt
that the musicians took all the fun out of singing by setting the notes on those stiff shelves. I accepted the
teacher's punishments, practising the scales for hours on
end, on my knees, and promising myself vengeance while
I put heart and soul into singing a song from Mindelo in
Cape Verde that cried out against cruel Fate. They
explained to me what would happen to a missionary
sent off to some far-flung parish with no musical training
for the ceremonies and prayers, with sharp-eared,
demanding, eccentric parish zealots always ready with
threats of papal bulls. And down below, in the seminary,
in that gleaming tin-roofed house, you heard the regular
tolling of the bells announcing the divisions of the day,
and the rich sounds of the harmoniums recalling the
innocence of limbo or the early days of paradise.

I devoted myself to sport, taking as my models not the gifted seminarians who became priests but those who had left the seminary to become brilliant basketball players in teams in Díli. I had forgotten my priorities, but a few bad marks on my reports brought me a paternal ultimatum telling me that this was the only place where I would have any chance of studying and that failure meant losing my vocation and compromising my whole future. A catastrophe for the family. It meant losing all hope, being plunged into the despair of life on the outskirts of Díli, joining the long list of those waiting for a job as a civil servant to come up or for the temporary salvation of military service. I concentrated harder on my studies, went on retreat and prayed fervently. My marks improved and with them my behaviour and, when the year was up, my vocation was confirmed. I was chosen for the seminary, with my future assured and my father's worries calmed. At last, I was in the eagle's nest, with a splendid veranda thick with bougainvillaea and a magnificent view over the city of Díli, the sea and, on the horizon, the island of Ataúro.

The teachers were all Jesuit priests. A mixture of Latins. Priests from Portugal and Spain and one from France, Father Bernard, who had been a lieutenant in the First World War and still had a sliver of grenade in his chest and the *Marseillaise* in his heart. He had turned priest and turned to China, which promptly

turned Communist and turned him out, but he religiously kept a mandarin goatee and the composed air of
a Buddha. He taught French and Mathematics and
sometimes Franco-Mathematics. I finally learned the
Latin I had so often mumbled my way through in
masses, litanies and Gregorian chants. It was my trump
card when I got into linguistic arguments with my brothers, who, at the time, dedicated themselves to flirting
with Australian tourists and trying out the delights of the
English language. The declensions came from the grammar book and the literary texts from Ovid and Virgil,
arma virunque cano. Some of the older priests took
pleasure in talking amongst themselves in that dead and
venerable language as if they had been reincarnated from
emperors, philosophers and eunuchs. They had the gift
of oratory, could write fluent, complex texts and were
noted for their rhetorical gestures and poses. Rarity
brings prestige, and, in the holidays, I used my skills as a
student of Latin to explain the origins of the Portuguese
words that my father looked up in a large dictionary.
Delighted, he would excitedly present me to his patients
as an added dimension to his services. He saved their
skins, and when he couldn't, I saved their souls.

The theatre was another regular activity, especially
the plays of Portuguese writers like Gil Vicente and José
Régio. Each week there was an evening of either singing
or poetry; some daring people even declaimed in public

the poems of Antero de Quental, poems that spoke of the poet's supreme doubts about the divine, to an audience of confirmed certainties and faith. Others excelled themselves writing magnificent sonnets of which I understood not a word, but from then on I began to divide men into those who wrote sonnets and those who wrote quatrains. We were taught to converse in various languages, to discuss ideas and to acquire a taste for reading and literature. There were evenings of art, classical music and films, and nights spent camping. We listened to records and to the voice of a priest singing poems by Sophia de Mello Breyner, 'We see, we hear, we read . . .'

Vietnam was just across the water, war was being waged in Angola and in Guinea-Bissau. Each year brought the departure of students who, having completed their secondary education in Timor, were going off to Portugal to study Philosophy and Theology. Each year saw the arrival of new priests, who, it was assumed, would brighten up the sombre daily lives of the natives; they were sent off into the interior, became lost in anonymity, never to be heard of again. In Díli, given the absence of eligible young men, former seminarians attracted a great deal of attention, for although not priests, they benefited from the aura of ostensible intellectualism, which I thought was exactly what had kept them from sacred office. They went on to occupy important posts in the administration of Timor, they published articles in the newspapers, taught in schools and married pretty, eye-catching women from the city. In Dare, people repeated in low voices the prayer of the old *matam-doc*, the visionary, who went to the prelate and said that he would like his son to be a father, but if that proved impossible, then he'd be quite happy for him to be a mother instead. It was at least a way out, an opportunity. However, when nothing ever came of that opportunity, the bishop rebelled against the governor, taking advantage of the liturgical celebrations for Nation Day, in the presence of the pretender to the throne of Portugal, to call for donations from the royal family and from the Bishop of Medeiros Foundation to provide bursaries for those who wanted to study in Portugal.

And from Portugal came the sports newspaper, *A Bola*, fought over by sports fanatics, who would learn the players' names by heart, causing the school's spiritual director to deliver homilies castigating seminarians who knew the names of all the footballers but not the names of saints. For good or ill, another paper, *A Época*, always ended up in the hands of those who argued about everything and nothing, and who found amusement and substance in the barrack-room quarrels of retired soldiers, in the replacement of retired ministers, and approved of the Holy Father giving an audience to retired terrorists, explaining that when it came to politics, the Holy Father did not necessarily always have recourse to his privilege or gift of infallibility. The magazine *Coral* was everyone's favourite. People tried out ideas there, published sonnets and quatrains, dedicated, in the absence of any real lovers, to some distant, female entity. I had a go at publishing a quatrain about the town of Lautém, describing it as white, naked and in the grip of madness. I was severely reprimanded; in my defence, I said only that it had too much substance and too few syllables.

I don't know quite what happened that year. It was the year of the purge. I was thirteen. I had passed the fourth year with decent marks, but was dismissed along with some fellow students who I thought were perfectly priestworthy: honest, studious and with modestly lowered eyes. For that year, despite the prospect of my family's distress at having bet on a horse that failed to last the distance, I pulled up short. I was about to enter a different race.

6

When I was a child, I was told to keep well away from the place where the rainbow begins, for it was said to be the lair of the boa constrictor, who after a sumptuous supper belched blurred bloodstains into the clouds tracing a reptilian curve across the sky.

I was afraid of the city of Díli, which had grown as bloated as a boa constrictor that has just swallowed a buffalo. It dragged its great belly through the outskirts. When I crossed the city, I felt like a mountain goat about to be gulped down like a kebab in the midst of that crush of buildings in the city centre, where the administrative offices were to be found, together with the schools, the Chinese shops and the public park full of bright red acacias, which also adorned the monument to the Discoveries, guarded by rusty old bits of artillery pointing out at the inert, vanquished wrecks of Japanese warships from the Second World War.

My father, now an old, weary nurse, had been transferred from the town of Lautém to help combat TB in the Lahane hospital. He worked in the sanatorium to which people with tuberculosis were exiled after long years of using betel juice to disguise the red blood they coughed up. He lived in Vila Verde, near the Kaikoli swamp which was carpeted with giant grasses and where the power station was hidden, and in which, so it was said, lurked spirits who kidnapped people taking the short cut to the market. Their bodies were flushed down the sewers and out into the sea.

Dilli, by contrast, was a noisy city full of public works vehicles with iron trailers attached, trawling the periphery. They belonged to the company known as the Agricultural Society of Fatherland and Work and carried ululating Firakus to the processing factory for the coffee brought from Ermera, land of the *calades*. Above all, though, it was a city full of shops owned by Chinese traders, who slept out the siesta with their doors wide open, and full of soldiers who, having no war to fight, wandered the beaches and the tarmac streets, not knowing what to do with themselves. The Portuguese soldiers dressed in civvies to go to the city, like people making constant pilgrimages to Our Lady of Healing. As well they might, this far from the wars being waged in the other Portuguese colonies. The coast road ran from one side of the city to the other, from the white wrought-iron streetlamp near where the military and civil authorities had their residences, past the port of Díli that smelled of sandalwood from the crates waiting to be loaded onto ships, to Lecidere and the streetlamp in the shape of a white candle, near the bishop's official residence. It continued as a dirt road that crossed the Bidau bridge, where the so-called 'local Portuguese' was spoken, to the beach of Areia Branca, refuge of clandestine lovers. Any woman seen coming back from there was deemed to be a fallen woman. And I would pretend to ignore the romantic faces of my female compatriots, who went from motorbike to motorbike, clinging to young Portuguese recruits – who had doubtless left girlfriends behind them in Lisbon – as if they were the last camels in the desert.

Díli was not a white city. Its glittering tin roofs scorched the air. In the late afternoon, it closed like a shining shell, and the evenings were sweet, with the island of Ataúro hunched like a sentinel on the horizon.

We all went to enrol in our new school together. A caravan – when I was younger, I would have called it a procession – to frighten away our own ghosts. Into the fifth year of secondary school and my fourteenth year. An elevated position, given the general academic level of the country, and one that would allow access to a good job on a plantation, the headship of an administrative post in some town in the interior, or training as an army sergeant, which would mean being saluted by one's inferiors and receiving a salary generous enough to buy a Honda 90 and to get oneself a well-educated girlfriend.

Awaiting us were the veterans, whose feverish, staring eyes promised us a life of misfortune and misery. We were the intruders, the trespassers on other people's property, and worse, those whom Fate had not chosen to follow the Way: we were failed priests. Some of the veterans – those who had to repeat their repeats – had become the guardians of that wretched temple, pinned down by its weight, year after year, to the same desk, and so they had put down roots. There was a high failure rate at the school for those living on the outskirts, for the nearby beach awarded its own certificate, their families were far away and their companions a very mixed bag. The school was highly selective and the children of European VIPs studied there. Still half asleep, they were brought to school in official cars and would be woken up in the classroom by the teachers, the wives of inferiors and subalterns, 'Did young Pedro not sleep well last night?' The sons of minor functionaries, from Europe or the colonies, who arrived in private cars, would be told, 'Pedro, be quiet!' And the sons of functionaries born in Timor, 'Listen, number 27, either you shut up or you're out!'

To me, in my moral superiority, the place had always seemed a den of iniquity. Although I was forced to moderate my views by the number of students who went on retreats to the seminary, I eyed them mistrustfully as if they were servants of the Devil granted leave of absence.

Later, I realized how few advantages the school now brought, despite the pretty girl students who wore brief white smocks that allowed a glimpse of white lace knickers and drew a large phalanx of 'cowboys' and bikers to parade up and down near the building. Once, it had been the only place that provided staff for the island's administration. The Portuguese Youth Movement had pitched camp there, and some students had made a career as commanders of *castelos*, or as bohemians and singers, who invented words in Tetum for English songs that lived on for ever in the hearts of lovers of *korem-metam* parties.

Hau hakerek surat ida . . .

I'm writing a letter . . .

Very few students reached the final year of secondary school and could dream of getting a scholarship to study in Portugal. Normally, they would leave when they were just old enough to join up or to get married. Given the high failure rate and the lack of career opportunities, a technical school was set up, named after the Foreign Minister of the day, Silva Cunha. It was a modern building that reminded me of a dovecote and which attracted a lot of young Timorese men, mainly from the interior. They were looking for short courses that would allow them to get a job. The Portuguese Youth Movement immediately changed headquarters, leaving the secondary school free for the activities of the man in charge of the ANP* – who just happened to be the headmaster – and thus separating off the political wing from the paramilitary wing, although both supported Salazar.

The governor of Timor at the time, Colonel Alves Aldeia, was the latest in a long line of military governors, even after the territory had been pacified. He was a tall, robust, energetic man, with a gift for fiery rhetoric to rival that of the bishop; he was also highly visible after the grey and brown figures who had previously adorned the palace. His mission and his desire was to drag Timor and the Timorese out of its oblivion as a dumping ground for subversives, and he visited every corner of the island, every town and village, sometimes by car, sometimes on horseback and often on foot. He crossed to Ataúro in a *corocora*, drawing attention to the fact that he was the only governor ever to have made such a visit. He met the local leaders and made a point of knowing all about any illnesses the chiefs of the *sukus* might be suffering and about the difficulties experienced by ordinary people. When he couldn't help, he would dip into the petty cash to give hand-outs here and there, silencing the complaints of the traditional leaders. He was very keen that his actions should be known about in Timor, publicized in Portugal, and compared with what

---

* The Associação Nacional Popular was the government party under the Salazar regime.

went on in Indonesian Timor which, at the time, was
less developed. He set up the newspaper *A Voz de Timor*
to promote his various activities, which were always
turned into solemn occasions, especially after the arrival
of a Timorese journalist trained in Mozambique and
who had reported on the war there. His name was José
Ramos-Horta and he had all the glamour of the war
correspondent. In fact, the governor was taking a small
revenge on the newspaper *A Seara* (*The Cornfield*),
owned by the diocese of Díli, and which had given voice
to local dissatisfactions in an article by one Ramos Paz
about the role of the native Timorese people. Now each
newspaper had its Ramos. The governor hoped that his
Ramos would challenge the bishop's Ramos – a palace
contest between two fighting cocks.

   Timor was living through its own age of discoveries.
Despite being an island in the back of beyond, ignored by
everyone, the outside world still entered the palm-
thatched houses. Nothing that went on abroad escaped
our notice, thanks to all those Australian tourists on their
pilgrimages to the tempting beaches of Bali and those
Australian broadcasting stations bombarding us with
news and banned songs. *A Seara* had opened its pages to
ex-seminarians, allowing them to try out various theories
beneath the fascinated gaze of their compatriots. They
defended the legitimacy of pagan marriages and of the
bride-price, which someone had had the audacity to

describe as evidence of our being a backward people. And when Ramos-Horta dared to pen an article for *A Seara* dedicated to Brother Maubere*, the governor seized the opportunity to silence the voice of the Church, and teach a bitter lesson to the editor of the suspended newspaper, Father Martinho Lopes, as he then was. It made no difference that he had been a deputy in the National Assembly in Portugal. And he was to suffer far worse treatment at the hands of the Indonesians, who expelled him from Timor – again it made no difference that, by then, he had been made a bishop. The governor felt that being betrayed by his own fighting cock – who had dared to change ownership – was the worst thing that could have happened to him, especially when he had lavished such care on him and had taken the trouble to see through the journalist's *kulit mahar*, or thick skin, to his talent as a writer. He responded harshly to the arrogance of his rival, Father Lopes, reducing him to silence, though sparing the cockerel, as would any true lover of the art. A man might lose a herd of buffalo, a field of rice, a coffee plantation, a house, a pearl necklace, gold, silver, women, his wife and his faith, but never a fighting cock!

---

* *Maubere* was originally used by the Mambae, one of the poorest hill people in Timor, to mean 'friend'. The Portuguese used it to mean backward and primitive, as a way of denigrating the Timorese peasantry. Fretilin made the word a symbol of what their movement represented: to be a *maubere* ('my brother or friend') was to be a son of Timor. It came to symbolize the reassertion of Timorese culture and the struggle against poverty and colonial subordination.

The tireless Alves Aldeia was creating what would later be thought of as an open governorship, taking as his aide-de-camp the cheerful, amusing Ângelo Correia, engineer and long-distance runner, and making him Head of Tourism, with predictions of a sparkling future. But everyone felt that the governor actually preferred the traditional authorities, considering himself to be amongst peers. He commissioned a Timorese artist to paint his portrait in oils wearing traditional dress and adopting an ancestral pose; he was the reincarnation of the great Lusitanian hero, Dom Aleixo Corte-Real. And the local leaders liked him. At least they seemed to. The governor of Indonesian West Timor was also a colonel, El-Tari. They exchanged visits, receptions, gifts and made promises of mutual respect. Sports teams and musical troupes from the Portuguese side visited the city of Kupang and returned overwhelmed by the friendliness of the rulers, the beauty of the women and the euphoric reception given by their neighbours to Portuguese folk-lore as interpreted by the Timorese. From the Indonesian side came elegant basketball players from Java, dancers from Bali and the famous singer from Surabaya, Ervina, who at the Santo António celebrations drove the enraptured, hysterical soldiers wild with her glossy, limber legs, which were as famous as her husky voice.

It was during that visit by El-Tari that pamphlets containing pro-Indonesian propaganda first appeared. We all knew of and talked in hushed tones about the events of 1959 that had deprived some Timorese families of their relatives, accused of leading a rebellion and sent into exile in Angola, Mozambique and the Azores. Although some Timorese had, in fact, benefited from the Portuguese presence, these others still nursed a healthy hatred of the colonial authorities. They felt it was the right moment to show themselves, albeit obliquely. El-Tari trusted Alves Aldeia. They were opposite numbers. And so as not to give rise to any malicious rumours that the two neighbours were excluding Australia – an attentive, perhaps interested observer, who had in the past even intervened – the city of Darwin also took an active part in this mini-ménage à trois.

Venâncio was the oldest amongst us in the secondary school and wore prescription glasses that made him look older still. He was the leader of a group of Dare rejects who retained the measured attitudes and gestures of someone performing sacramental duties. He cycled to school on an old black bike which he had acquired, sixth hand, from a junk dealer, an exile from Macau. Some made fun of him, saying that he would make it to the scrap heap even before the bike, a vehicle which made as much of a racket as the hunk of horseflesh saved from the knacker's yard by Venâncio's classmate Adriano. Adriano was the only horseman in the school, a solitary figure; the whole city, however, was a park for self-styled lone horsemen, some on foot, some on bicycles, in imitation of the films shown at the only cinema, O *Sporting*, which showed westerns starring Trinita and romantic comedies featuring the Italian Gianni Morandi, whose song *Non sono digno de te* blared from the radio every night.

We had all agreed and sworn that none of us would renounce the old ways. The methods of study and discipline acquired during our years in the seminary would prove trump cards in the future and a guarantee of success, as already attested by others who, rejected by the seminary, had gone on to be brilliant students. We just had to follow in their footsteps. The novelty lay in the fact that, from then on, we would share the classroom not with images of protective patron saints, which each of us used to place in our desks in the hope of enlightenment, but with fellow students who gossiped about our immaturity when it came to certain matters to which some were devoted subscribers. But my father's orders had been forthright and conclusive. There was the cockpit and I had to be a prize rooster ready to do battle and not allow myself to be distracted by the feathers of the other cockerels. The fact that Timorese students had gone to Portugal on scholarships after secondary school made my progenitor forget the shame of my exclusion from clerical life and pin all his hopes on me as a route, via the airport, out of Timor, a reward for all the years of penury he had endured – the glory of having a son living overseas would recover his loan. I had read the same emotions on the faces of the parents of those who had already left. I went to the airport to wave off a student whom we ex-seminarians had once thought of as an *enfant terrible*. He had a highly developed musical sense and, so it was said, unusual intelligence. His name was Abílio Araújo. He was a short, fat, smiling lad, with all the poise of an administrator and the pomp of a ruler. People said that Alves Aldeia, his patron, had promised him a post in the Economics department. He was the great hope of those in government, but also of all his ancestors who wanted to see one of their children take up a responsible post in the running of the island*. That was when I realized that the person who got all the glory was the person who stayed behind. The fighting cock's owner was the real winner.

These fighting cocks often had mixed pedigrees and fortunes. Around that time, a certain Mário Carrascalão returned from the glory of Portugal, where he had gone to study forestry, and was appointed to the Ministry of Agriculture and Forestry. He was the son of old Carrascalão, originally from the Algarve, whose great

---

* One of the founders of Fretilin, Araújo became its leader in exile in Lisbon. In the late 1980s he changed sides and became a vocal supporter of the Indonesian occupation.

height made up for his limp and crippled hand, injuries
he had sustained during the anti-Salazar anarchist activities for which he had been exiled to Timor. He had
married a local woman, became a prosperous coffee-
grower, a respected citizen and was later rehabilitated by
the powers-that-be and made President of the town
council in Díli. Timor had a way of calming turbulent
spirits. Another son, Manuel Carrascalão, was chosen by
the Timor administration as the ANP candidate for the
National Assembly. At the ceremony the authorities were
asked by the journalist Ramos-Horta if, in the event of
an opposition candidate's coming forward, they would
give that candidate financial support to go and take
part in the opposition congress in Portugal. Everyone
assumed that the reply would be an order to arrest that
journalist, so fond of subversive games. Alves Aldeia
merely said that the government did not subsidize sub-
version, thus letting the journalist off lightly and
condemning Carrascalão, the official candidate, to exile
in Portugal. For Manuel Carrascalão was duly chosen as
candidate and – or so we found out later – apparently
ordered to be quiet when making a speech in the
Portuguese parliament. Some thought this an insult,
adding that it showed great ignorance, given that he was
the representative of the most far-flung outpost of the
empire, where the myth of *mate-bandera-hum* lingered
on with the blood of native heroes like Dom Jeremias de

Luca and Dom Aleixo Corte-Real. Others said that a religious figure would have coped better with such parliamentary clashes, someone wise and educated like Father Jorge Duarte or Father Martinho Lopes. Always neglectful of her maternal responsibilities to Timor, Portugal at this time behaved like a wicked stepmother.

The youngest son, João Carrascalão, returned from Angola where he had gone to study its topography. He was tall like his father, well-built like his mother and had grown stout on foreign beer, Cuca from Angola and Laurentina from Mozambique. He was accompanied by Mari Alkatiri, another promising young man, who came from the Arab community and who had once defied everyone's expectations by going on retreat at the seminary in Dare: a Muslim pondering the monastic hordes while the flag of the Crusades flew over this remote Jesuit stronghold built on the very fringes of the Crescent Moon. He had brothers studying at the same school as me who were said to possess magic charms or potions with a wide variety of uses; for example, they had an elixir for the brain which was made by relatives who came from Arabia. At exam time, they were besieged by those students who were repeating the year yet again. The topographical duo took to driving slowly along the coast road in bright red convertibles with their film-star beautiful girlfriends. Proudly, I watched them go by and dreamed of the time when I would be given a post in a

GALWAY COUNTY LIBRARIES

ministry, with a car straight out of a movie and a girl-friend who turned heads. Native Timorese people were being appointed to government posts. Study was the number one priority if we were to prove wrong the famous prelate who once said that Timor was more suited to the pickaxe than the pen.

In class, Venâncio, who wielded a very skilful pen, displayed his rare talent as a decliner of Latin nouns and a connoisseur of Platonism and the complicated *magna mater* complexes of Fernando Pessoa, Alexandre Herculano, Zarathustra and Camões. In the intimacy of his home, like a finicky archaeologist, he would search through his notes from the seminary for abstruse words with which to embellish his essays, which he would then diligently read out in class, freeing the rest of us from other tasks and making the blonde teacher blush at the seductive charm of the subjects broached, for his essays always closed with a reference to the eternal pursuit of happiness. And Happiness wore her long, dark hair in plaits; she hunched up her shoulders and angrily chewed her lips, embarrassed by this artisan of words and by the lack of any proper explanation. She did not expect such daring from a former would-be priest, someone who should be equally scholastic when it came to love. She did not feel it right that he should make such a public display – a display that also exposed her – of a subject which should, in principle, begin with sly exchanges of glances, suspicions, the filching of handkerchiefs and, finally, clandestine letters, not essays addressed to no one in particular and which proved more successful in seducing the teacher than in seducing Happiness herself. And at the end of the school year, Venâncio, lost in the meanderings of others' complexes, had still not found happiness. He had, however, discovered the idea of Charon and the crossing. He applied for a scholarship and sailed the seven seas to take a course in Land Management at the University of Évora.

Adriano would enter the classroom with slow, solemn steps as if he were still mounted on his horse. He had the look of John Wayne and the walk of Trinita, and would be whistling the theme tune of his favourite film between his teeth. In his imagination he was always wearing cowboy gear even when he was, in fact, wearing shiny, terylene trousers, since he lacked the money to pay the inflated prices demanded by the Filipino sailors from the merchant ship *Musi* for the smuggled jeans they sold on the Díli quayside. Adriano had fallen in love with Fernanda, who sat in front of him in class, allowing the horseman to ponder with eyes, hands, body and soul the cataract of long, dark hair that fell down her back. Fernanda, however, was spoken for, though not according to her parents. Her boyfriend, a police officer, eventually kidnapped her, leaving her chair empty and Adriano gazing into the infinite and cursing his fate.

After all, he was the cowboy and, morally speaking, he should have been the one to do the kidnapping.

That year, my father embarked for Singapore to take care of the crew on the *Arbiru* and promised me that if on his return I had done well in my studies, he would pay for me to modernize myself from head to toe. And so it came to pass. He let me grow my hair long and took me to a Chinese tailor who made me a pair of bell-bottoms that dragged along the ground as if my legs were employed as walking brooms. What saved me were the accessories – Cuban-heeled shoes that my father had bought especially for me in Singapore as a New Year present and which gave me an airy visibility. I could enjoy the limpid breeze blowing in from the sea; wearing my Cuban heels was like living on the third floor in a ground-floor city. But nothing escaped the sharp eyes of those who take pleasure in others' misfortunes. They turned their fire on me and marked my brow with a name that still lingers today amongst Timorese people, even those born after I left Timor: *Takas* or High Heels. It sounds like some kind of ancient car which was, like me, very slow to accelerate.

At the end of secondary school, apart from Venâncio and the other students who left for Portugal, some marked time before joining up and others tried their luck in the civil service. My age, sixteen, and my father's plans for me precluded either of those two options. Having enrolled for the sixth form, I thus became one of the half-dozen students who dreamed of going on to higher education in Portugal, assuming that the governor continued his policy of training potential Timorese staff by giving out scholarships. Around that time, a few young army officers arrived from Portugal, mostly drafted into the army as a punishment for their political activities at university, whose wives taught at our school and armed me with a knowledge of clandestine literature. They described the University of Coimbra with its serenades, *fados* and its special student customs, they talked about the Académica football team, about the student protests when the President of the Republic visited Coimbra in 1969. At one time, at night, I used to read the Bible out loud by the light of the kerosene lamp, but now, in the early hours of the morning, by torchlight, I secretly devoured *Black Skin, White Masks* by Frantz Fanon and *The Mother* by Gorky. I felt different after reading these books, not so much, as with the Biblical stories, because of the spell they cast, but because of the shame surrounding these secret sessions. I remember a teacher of philosophy talking about her husband, a captain in the army, and saying how sick he was of the war, having been sent to the battle front in place of others who remained in the safety of the rearguard. For the first time, native ears heard the complaints of someone whose mission until then had been to seduce and charm. Timor made a good rearguard.

The army continued its morale-raising campaign amongst the soldiers not at war, who were stationed all over the island doing things like building schools for young Timorese with no money to pay for their studies. It recruited anyone with talent, whether Portuguese or Timorese (who were occasionally to be found scattered throughout various barracks) – romantic singers and would-be bandits who laid down their rifles and, arming themselves with a guitar and a microphone, set off in a so-called artistic troupe, rather like one of those travelling shows in a pulp western. It was certainly the only time that people would hear banned songs by the likes of Zeca Afonso (*Grândola, vila morena*) sung by student officers, or popular songs and dance tunes and António Mafra (. . . *eram prà aí sete e picos*) sung by soldiers from provincial folk clubs, and a woman's orgasmic moans imitated by a male singer, a frequenter of Lisbon discotheques, in a rendition of *Je t'aime moi non plus*.

Even more daringly, they showed films in the barracks, for adults of all ages, films never shown at the local cinema. On these occasions, the barracks' doors were opened to the female substratum of the population. We had no alternative but to make minor military incursions of our own, crawling under the barbed wire, while the guards were savouring the perfume of these rare visitors. The flesh is weak, even when armed with iron. Lying on the droppings left by the herds of pigs foraging for the soldiers' leftovers, I first saw the magnificent actress who was to me as delightful as a rare bird, and frightening too: she was the image of Pontiana. Vanessa Redgrave was the perfect embodiment of Isadora Duncan, the American dancer, as she fell in love with a Russian poet who drank vodka, took part in the revolution and said he wanted them to make love like two tigers. I began to have my doubts as to whether that particular communist had, in fact, ever eaten children. At any rate, I liked that free spirit with eyes the colour of the sea, so like the American anthropologist who visited my house and was going to study Mambae in Same. She chewed betel and talked with the tonic stress of the *calades*, substituting fs for ps and causing general hilarity. There were other anthropologists besides her, interested in matters we thought irrelevant and unimportant, since we had only ever studied things that came from the other side of the world.

With the installation of electricity in the city, the violinist Abril Metam very nearly lost his glamour, but, cast out into the periphery, he gained in prestige at the *korem-metam* parties, which were still held by the light of kerosene lamps. Electricity allowed for innovation. Groups playing electrified instruments sang rock songs and jitterbugged, although Timorese couples – the women wearing traditional dress – continued to dance cheek to cheek, even when the noise reached an earsplitting peak. There were Cinco do Oriente and Ué-Lulik who imitated Credence Clearwater Revival, the Rolling Stones and the Beatles, and sang a few Timorese songs set to a new beat. We had only ever heard Amália, the voice of *fado*, on the radio until one day she decided to come to Timor and sing for the Timorese people – not that we ever actually got a chance to see the sad, yearning face of *fado*. The authorities closeted themselves up with her in such a tiny venue that they almost succeeded in suffocating her. It was as though they wanted to hide from native eyes and ears the voice of this bewitching soul who might reveal to us the true aims of the Discoveries. Later, after protests from the singer, they presented a weary, distracted Amália to a stadium still empty of native Timorese. I sought comfort in conjuring up memories of my classmate, who, skinny as his father, Master Egídio from the school in Soibada, used to fill his lungs with air and then release it in long exhalations, the words pouring from his mouth like a cascade – '*Povo que lavas no rio*', 'People of Portugal, you who wash in the river.' At the time, unaware that the Tagus flowed right through Lisbon, I thought that such a river would have to be the size of the sea.

From time to time, young men as pale as kapok would leave the Lisbon docks on the *Timor* and be deposited on the quayside at Díli, where the ship would pick up others, burned more by the passage of time than by the sun, leaving behind them my downcast female compatriots from both halves of the country – Loro Monu in the west and Loro Sae in the east – who had dressed hurriedly in awkward miniskirts, in order to hear the song of the siren on the quayside:

Malae bá ona!

The foreigner is leaving.

My brother Toni already spoke good English, acquired in his work as a headstrong, enthusiastic tour guide. He formed a duo with Carlos Campara and both promised to introduce me to the sweet domain of worldly pleasures. According to one, learning a language always began with initiation rites involving certain physical activities. The other added that he found it more enjoyable talking to women in a foreign language like French. He would say to me, *'Je t'aime moi non plus*,' and then stop, his eyes closed. The rest, he concluded, was just Latin, like when the priests said mass.

Toni was the one who deciphered the words of songs from LPs for the lead singer of Cinco do Oriente. The Australian firm, the Broken Hill Proprietary Company, prospecting in Betano, Alas and Suai, asked him to work for them. He was old enough to do his military service and was plotting with some Australian girlfriends how to escape Timor. Although he had the robust physique of a boxer, he did not feel sufficiently patriotic to don a uniform. A few veiled threats from sergeants, who said they

were looking forward to seeing him at the training centre
in order to settle a few scores, only confirmed his belief
that it would be best to make a run for it. A lot of young
men in Díli dreamed of doing the same. But another
brother, named after the prophet Ananias, grew tired of
city life and, responding to the call of communal ties,
went back to our homeland of Manufahi and married a
local woman of the same blood, in accordance with all
the traditional marriage rituals, including the payment of
a bride-price.

The family was purging itself of neutral non-native
elements and fortifying itself behind the rigid structures
of alliances and oaths.

My awareness of my own sins and a permanent readi-
ness for self-criticism made me something of a crybaby.
I cried when I heard about the ship going down. If it had
happened a year earlier, I would have lost my father. It
looked like a ship built to see off monsoons and pirates,
as its name confirmed: it was called *Arbiru* after the
Portuguese lieutenant who had starved out the people of
Cailaco when they took refuge in the hills to avoid
paying their tribute money. I should have wept with joy
that the gods had finally, albeit tardily, taken their
revenge on this name. No misfortune ever bound a
people more closely to their masters – it seems the ship
had gone to the bottom with a precious cargo, the wives
of the top brass on their way to Singapore to do some

shopping. The story of the sole survivor swelled the sales of *A Voz de Timor*, and although the chief meteorologist tried to come up with a scientific explanation, producing a diagram which showed the eye of the storm coinciding with the path of the *Arbiru*, there were gleeful whispers offering alternative, less natural explanations: 'Pirates to the port side!'

Once tears had dried, the governor set off for consultations in Portugal. The uprising of 16 March 1974* almost caught him in Lisbon and prevented him from returning to Timor. When he did return, the whole city turned out to greet him, and he, overwhelmed by the reception, was bullish about the future. He gave a fiery speech, berating all those who dared to question the nation's destiny and who belonged to a body of which he was the legitimate representative in Timor. It was the swan song of the governor or *liurai mutim*, the white tribal leader, and of an imperial age that was drawing to a close on Ramelau**. Shortly afterwards, the revolution of 25 April took place in Portugal.

---

* The date of an army officers' uprising in the town of Caldas da Rainha in Portugal. It failed, but was followed shortly afterwards by the successful revolution of 25 April.

** Ramelau was the highest peak in the Portuguese empire. The Tetum name, Tatamailau, means 'grandfather of mountains' and Fretilin adopted it as a symbol of the high aspirations of the Timorese people.

7

The old nurse, my father, had told me that the shipwreck of the *Arbiru* was a portent of catastrophe. So accustomed was he to reading the fates and fortunes of men in the changing weather and in the songs of birds, that, after that fateful day, he never had a moment's peace. He cried bitterly over the tragic event, remembering the times when he had shared with the sailors the rise and fall of the waves, the threat of monsoons, the falling stars and the beautiful women of Singapore. But the intensity of his grief made me think that he must be weeping over something far darker, which I guessed was unease about the future. He used to say that success at school could give me the opportunity of exile from Timor on merit. This time, that advice had the force of an exclusion order. So when the actual moment of the catastrophe came, I would be far away and unable to share it with him – but he was already prepared for any difficulties.

News of the April revolution was broadcast on the radio, and the communiqués issued by the Council of National Salvation in Lisbon seemed like just another football report, listened to eagerly for the results. Football was the only constant link between the mother country and far-flung colony, especially since the departure of a Timorese player, Pincho, for the Belenenses football club.

Everything in Timor continued as before. The governor drove down in his official car from his residence at the top of Lahane, and was greeted by native guards at the entrance to the palace. The authorities continued to produce documents, and the civil servants awaited their salary at the end of the month. No one ran out into the streets crying 'Freedom!', no one unfurled the old subversive flags. It was as if Timor were repaying Portugal in kind for all those long years of neglect and indifference. Although we all knew that the routine of daily life could not last much longer, no one dared to question it. We had to savour it, down to the last drop.

The revolution had been led by army captains and so it fell to their counterparts in Timor to spread the revolution there. However, in the barracks our captains merely pretended that nothing had changed; they received the salutes of the privates and the confidences of the majors and waited for some decree from Lisbon that would officially mark the end of the regime. Some feared that the army staff was waiting for the publication of the speech given by the governor on his return from Portugal so that, with that incriminating evidence in their hands, they could call for his dismissal.

'How could he be so foolish!' my father asked me, surprised by the brevity of the gap between the moment that the winds of change started blowing and the governor's delivery of that final speech, whose content had been disguised by the applause of those present and those absent. He was both concerned and curious to find out what would emerge. In moments of depression, he suspected that those in power were engaged in some kind of ritual of expiation. The governor was still professing his faith in eternal life when he knew perfectly well God had decided that man would die of cancer. Every concubine fears her man will want to leave, but he, in the interests of status and propriety, kept us hanging on, never saying when he would be going. And when he did go, he simply closed the door behind him without bolting it, to indicate that he would return, even though he knew he would not.

Public oratory was one thing; gloomy, Sebastianist mysteries were quite another. My father said that Timor's fate was being decided as if by divine mandate: the people had placed themselves in God's hands. It didn't matter whether the left or the right won. What their ears had heard was the exuberance of the words, not the content of the speech. So he kept silent and withdrew from the family to think, shutting himself up in the sanatorium with his patients. He waited anxiously for the publication of the governor's whole speech on the front page of *A Voz de Timor*, which was where the words and actions of governors were usually recorded. He went back to reading the big dictionary to decipher the words heard over the crackling radio, as if they were coffee beans defecated by a palm civet. Alves Aldeia disappointed everyone's expectations – it was his revenge, knowing that someone was after his post. Still in full exercise of the mandate conferred by the old regime and maintained by Portugal's distance and indifference, he appointed himself his own censor, enraging all those who hoped for scornful words aimed at those who had overturned order and been acclaimed in the streets of Lisbon, and who, clutching a new mandate, finally entered the palace and demanded that the governor surrender his power. Others, crestfallen, waited for the publication of the speech, as a reaffirmation of values accumulated over the centuries and which could not be called into question just like that. The governor had been responsible for inculcating many of those values and surely could not simply flee his responsibilities without disappointing the whole of history.

The newspaper made no mention of the speech or the warm welcome. Nothing happened. The lion's roar turned out to be a death rattle. He, the last governor, had relinquished the responsibility inherited from the early years of the colony's establishment and from the few years in which he had been a protagonist and had won the affection of the people and made allies of the traditional chiefs. Prudently, he broke that *quello* or alliance bracelet. He thus excluded himself from being the lone man against history, like the sole survivor of the *Arbiru*, whose story Alves Aldeia had questioned: he would rather have seen him go under, as he himself did.

About then, the *Timor* arrived at Díli quayside, having followed the same route as the caravels of the Portuguese discoverers. For some, this was a guarantee that what had happened was a mere farce, or a prank designed to alarm the unwary. If the revolution was a *fait accompli*, wondered others, what were those young recruits doing there, having travelled for forty days, their bodies salty from the sea winds, if they were not going to test out their hard, sinewy muscles in that hot, humid land? They were more like exiles than crusaders. They were meant to oversee the continuing discoveries – in lands which, according to Camões in *The Lusiads*, that great epic of the Discoveries, are the first to see the sun when it rises and are the source of shiploads of healthful, sweet-smelling sandalwood – but were arriving at the very moment when the cycle of empire had come to a close and the resurrection and later death of this new nation were just beginning. What would they do in this land, if the task that had brought them there had been cancelled by those who had trained them? The news spread rapidly that the *lírios* or lilies, as the new recruits were called, did not want to leave the ship, since their mission was at an end. A war that had never even started was over. They wanted to go home, as if they had merely traced the footsteps of the discoverers, their predecessors. Other passengers, suitcases ready, were strangely uneuphoric about their own homecoming. Did they have some inkling about what was going to happen to Timor? What enigma silenced the siren song of *malae bá ona*? It seemed that freedom had faded along with the farewell.

In Timor, no one expected that these sudden events would find the Timorese and their elite ready to assume responsibilities. The general feeling was that what had happened had little to do with the interests of Timor and everything to do with the interests of Portugal and the larger colonies currently engaged in wars of independence. Under Alves Aldeia, Timor was just beginning an era like the one brought about by the colonial wars in the other Portuguese territories. Many Timorese students were studying in Portugal and others would follow; there they could make use of their school manuals and travel through the land of Almeida Garrett.

Although the programme of the Armed Forces Movement – which overthrew the Caetano government on 25 April 1974 – encouraged the formation of other political parties, no one wanted to take the first step. Everyone knew who was who, their private dissatisfactions and their public desires. I knew, or at least I thought I knew, the secret thoughts of my compatriots, whom I imagined to be grouped according to their major interests and minor ambitions. The most obvious, because the nearest, was that small group of civil servants and night-school students who gathered at the *korem-metam* parties, in cafés and public parks and who, under cover of the sexist comments they directed at the better-looking female passers-by, composed remarks about the miniskirt of international politics and the négligé of domestic politics. Some were married, others were devoured by celibacy, and others still were merely amusing, perverse revellers. They shared a distant hope and while they awaited its realization, they made wild statements in the newspapers, participated in religious experiences and adopted passing fads. They had gone beyond the euphoric hippy phase, had abandoned long hair, bell-bottoms and Cuban heels. They plunged into the sea of internalized rebellion. They were immaculate in well-pressed clothes, they smelled of camphor and eau de Cologne. Although the fashionable stance was one of rebellion, some of these people were excellent timekeepers – civil servants with promising careers, people from established families, with children and responsibilities into the bargain. They awaited the descent from the heavens of those who had received scholarships to Lisbon and were thought of as the leaders of the future, albeit masked by distance, but who had meanwhile

aligned themselves with extreme left-wing student move-
ments which kept them supplied with pamphlets and
ideology.

They were all so very different. There was the extro-
vert journalist Ramos-Horta, who, by then, was already
involved in foreign affairs, namely the female companions who, on starry nights on the beach at Areia Branca,
like guardian angels, provided him with juicy bits
of information. Another was the severe, introverted
ex-seminarian Nicolau Lobato, who dressed almost
monastically, read voraciously and wrote in a firm hand
with a fountain pen. Accustomed in his earlier life to
carrying around the prayer book and the Bible, he always
walked through Díli with a book under his arm (doubtless philosophy or the social sciences) apparently deep in
thought, as if he had found an internal oasis and had
decided to stay there. He was the son of Master Narciso
from Soibada, the same one who used to go hunting and
make me dream of more nourishing meals. Both Ramos-
Horta and Nicolau Lobato had studied at the same
school – Nuno Álvares Pereira. Both had learned
Portuguese with the help of whacks from a cane and had
been fed on a diet of maize. After primary school,
Ramos-Horta, a barefoot *malae oan**, endowed with a
naturally subversive turn of mind, could not face being

---

* Tetum expression for the son of a white (i.e. Portuguese) foreigner.

shut up in a seminary again and went to the secondary
school in Díli, where he continued to exercise the genius
for revolt inherited from his father, who had been exiled
to Timor for anti-Salazar activities. As the son of a catechism teacher, Nicolau grew up with the creed on his
lips and a rosary in his hand and went straight to the
seminary, pre-programmed for great sacrifices and the
renunciation of the temporal world. Even now I cannot
understand how the Church threw away such talent and
religious feeling yet kept others who were mere cele-
brants of the liturgy. These two poles, one extremely
worldly, the other profoundly religious, formed the
embryo of a nationalist party, presented for the first time
coolly and ingenuously by Ramos-Horta in the building
belonging to the ACAIT (Commercial, Agricultural and
Industrial Association of Timor). Manuel Carrascalão,
the sacked deputy, was there too, convinced, finally, that
only democracy would allow him to speak freely. He sat
down in a large chair and listened to the words of
Ramos-Horta as he did his best to convince those present. He did so with such zeal, however, staring
particularly hard at the ex-deputy, that Carrascalão felt
offended. Once everyone had calmed down, Carrascalão,
without even mentioning Ramos-Horta's speech, claimed
that he too wanted independence, but that it was a far-off
goal somewhere in the infinite distance.

Manuel was from a large family whose members were

notable for height and physical strength. Although his father, a political deportee, had suffered greatly at first and had been exiled to Ataúro – Manuel was actually born on the crossing – he became a kind of born-again settler and his family grew wealthy. Other Portuguese settlers had stayed on after their military service and married native women and been given privileged access to government jobs. No white foreigner, historically speaking a guest, ever experienced hostility in Timor merely because they lived better than the people actually born there. It was logical, though, that with the regime gone they should feel that their possessions and pleasures were under threat, even though all that the forgotten, subordinated classes wanted were improved living conditions and a little respect: many of the privileges enjoyed by foreigners had been guaranteed by the mother country, now turned wicked stepmother and bearer of orphans. It was natural too that those Timorese educated in missionary schools according to the Christian model and later employed in the civil service were not prepared to give up what they had won; however tiny their salaries, they did, at least, guarantee sustenance for their numerous children. They said they were perfectly happy with things as they were, and opposed those who felt Timor should join Indonesia, whose neighbouring province was suffering terrible penury. They argued that, as a free nation, they could demand compensation from Portugal for its years of absence and neglect by creating a government administration with Timorese people trained in Portugal. That was my father's view, which is why he joined the UDT sympathizers. He dreamed that, one day, I would take up a post in that administration – the dreams of someone who has built a boat and wants to go on sailing through time, along the lost route of the colonizing caravels.

Others had gone to study philosophy and theology at the university in Macau, but had long since returned to Timor. They had decided not to become priests, but their bodies were still steeped in holy water and smelled of incense and vestments. They retained their angelic look, but were free now from any sacramental ties. They looked like small birds ready to soar with the wings of a hawk. They were philosophers, theologians, Latinists, Hellenists, but, above all, ex-seminarians. They came from the interior of Timor, born and raised in an indigenous environment in which the sacred presided over all everyday actions, thus providing the missionaries with fertile ground in which to plant their new religious influence. From worshipping stones to worshipping statues was but a step. They had studied at the missionary schools, where some of them had fathers who were catechism teachers. These schoolmasters, respected for their learning in the old knowledge, were also disseminators of Portuguese doctrine and grammar. They mixed the

pillars of native wisdom with Lusitanian allegory. When
their ex-pupils returned from Macau's capital, the City
of the Holy Name of God, they found jobs in public
administration, with a preference for the Customs and
Excise department where they were considered to be
superior civil servants and where they wore a white uniform laden with insignia. Some people were destined to
bend their backs, others merely to bend their heads. I
had heard their names, as distant as those of saints,
when I was a student at Soibada. I had learned to play
with certain words beginning with P, because of one seminarian in particular whose name was Pedro Paulo Pires,
a Portuguese painter who had been given permission to
pursue his painting in Portugal. I still await the return of
that painter, fixed in my imagination.

I had heard Xavier's illustrious name long before I
ever saw him. I knew that he had married the daughter
of Master Fernando from Soibada. Later, I glimpsed him
in Díli when he was dozing on the 500cc motorbike
that he used to transport the family on evenings out and
on which he sped off on night-time escapades in search
of *korem-metam* parties, perched awkwardly on the
saddle as if riding bareback on a horse. Xavier had a big
head, which my father told me was just like a saucepan,
his brain bubbling with intelligence. He never sweated.
His activity was solely intellectual. When the heat grew
oppressive, my father would begin to curse, inveighing

against that genius wasting his talent when so many people had none. Xavier had a hard face, a small moustache, like a screen hiding his knowing smile, and he corralled his small, shifty eyes behind thick-rimmed prescription glasses. He wrote better than he spoke. Anyone who had been wronged or had had their rights trampled upon would ask him to write their letters of complaint. He was a lawyer without a gown, and feared for his pen, which he wielded like a sword. He was loved and adored by his compatriots. When he opened an alternative secondary school in his house – where he taught wearing a sarong – for those who had dropped out of primary school and been rejected by the official secondary school, he had to plead *numerus clausus*, given the number of applications from beach *vanguardistas*.

His brother-in-law, Osório Soares, was short and light-skinned like his mother, but all he had inherited from his father, Master Fernando, was his curly hair. He was the chief of an administrative post by merit and by right, using the position as a horse upon which he rode in order to tilt at windmills. And like Cervantes' Don Quixote, he sported a long, flowing moustache. Everyone knew that he had been the one to distribute pro-Indonesian leaflets at the time of El-Tari's visit, as a way of avenging himself on the colonial authorities for exiling his uncle to the Azores. One assumes this was merely a passing tantrum since he had received a Catholic education in Soibada, had been confirmed in Aitara, used the Portuguese language correctly and, more than that, was married to a daughter of the former governor, Óscar Ruas. Never having found himself, he set out to find a windmill to fight. The horseman bringing war and death would be sure to follow.

The Lopes da Cruz brothers were always secondary figures in my daily life, given the unbearable presence of the oldest brother, Master Jaime. They were the sons of Master Humberto, a giant of a man who could bend metal with his bare hands. Mariano, back from Macau, spoke on the local radio station in a slow, Cantonese accent. I could feel his pleasure when, on his music programme, his voice would rise in uttering passionate dedications to the enchanted princess who lived on China Rate, or else issued a dread warning to the other lone horsemen prowling the area of Santa Cruz. There was no better way of going to sleep on Sunday afternoons than listening to the radio. Sometimes instead of the insults usually proffered by Jaime Neves – the official announcer and a fan of Sporting football club – one would hear Mariano's tender descriptions of the various moves, as if he were reading the Epistles, or hear him listing the names of the players as if they were the saints of the litanies. I would add an *ora pro nobis* to some of these homages and fall asleep. Francisco had inherited his father's athletic build and in Dare was more of a basketball player than a seminarian. He was the only one who could dunk the ball. His political skills were rather less appreciated. In Mozambique, he became an officer in the army, returning to Timor with a reputation as a fighter of terrorists. When he had done his military service, he donned the uniform of the Customs and Excise department and joined Domingos Oliveira from the neighbouring region of Laclubar. As his name suggests, there was something very Mediterranean about Oliveira, and the white uniform gave him the look of an Arab warrior riding a camel and taking tea in the desert. His large, round face reminded me of a painting of Abraham about to carry out God's orders and sacrifice his only son. He slumbered in the shade of his own name. No one took any notice of him, until one day he turned up with the statutes of the UDT in his hand and began writing the party's communiqués in a style reminiscent of the Mediterranean classics of philosophy. Thus one of the great Timorese thinkers woke from his long siesta. He had kept himself for the moment when he could prove most useful. He joined forces with Francisco Lopes da Cruz, and, assisted by Paulo Pires, the one I imagined as a painter, together they constituted the UDT trinity from Soibada.

Xavier do Amaral was chosen as the face of the ASDT

(Timorese Social Democratic Association) because of his rustic, ancestral profile and his aura of Western culture. All he lacked was ideological consistency. Nicolau Lobato gave him responsibility and lucidity, and Ramos-Horta international visibility. And thus Soibada also spawned the nationalist troika.

Osório Soares, still looking for windmills in the hope of being dubbed a knight, founded Apodeti (Timorese Popular Democratic Movement), who supported integration with Indonesia, drawing on his immediate family and relatives, exiled, dead or alive. With his brother-in-law, Domingos Pinto, also newly arrived from Macau, they formed the Apodeti duo.

Time was passing much too quickly, and the ancient current finally slipped over a steep precipice. In order to seize the moment, everyone wanted to move as fast as possible, faster even than time allowed. From being diverse factions, they became political rivals. How could they possibly have concealed so many contradictions? How was it possible for the tree of Samoro to have produced three such antagonistic branches?

At first, party communiqués were full of adjectives, metaphorical and inert. Once the writers realized that words could be more agitating than mosquito bites, and knowing how emotional the Timorese can be, they ransacked every dictionary and philosophical compendium they could find. Party broadcasts, at first rather like light entertainment programmes, became more like Jaime Neves' football commentaries, doling out insults to players, referees and anyone else involved. The radio guerrilla war broke out. The ex-seminarians tried out new catechisms on new sinners, whether communists, fascists or renegades.

Then the Lisbon students returned to Timor for a well-deserved holiday. They had not finished their degrees, but they came with plenty of practical experience acquired in student canteens and associations. They were the new wave, bringing with them whatever was currently in vogue. They did not look like colonial administrators and they cultivated the dishevelled mien of revolutionaries. They had left Timor in suits and ties and returned almost barefoot, causing one old catechism teacher to declare sadly that all his efforts had been in vain, that it would have been better if they had never gone to university but stayed in Timor to cultivate the ricefields of Natar Boro. My father advised me not to return in the same state; if I did, he would receive me with all the curses traditionally reserved for ungrateful sons.

Venâncio also returned in order to spend his holiday preaching politics in Timor. Instead of going to Macau, Timorese seminarians went to Évora in Portugal, which someone had told me was an ancient city, both Roman and Catholic. Now it also welcomed Timorese scholarship holders who, having completed secondary school,

chose to study Land Management. That decided
Venâncio's fate, vestments notwithstanding. He returned
from Portugal completely changed. His hunched body
had become erect and his docile face had become hard-
ened by the firmness of a new conviction. Accustomed to
being on the receiving end of doctrines, he assimilated
the new one with the same intensity with which he had
rejected the old. He was no longer the Platonist who
used to try to persuade catechumens of the need for res-
ignation, arguing the existence of an extraterrestrial
paradise; now this hard-line militant wanted to impose a
belief in an earthly paradise, tested and proved fruitful in
other latitudes under a different name and open to all
those who had been marginalized. What was at issue
here was not personal pride, but the pride of the people,
formerly known as one's fellow man. Perhaps he was
carrying the same flag as he had when, as a seminarian
with a handbell, he used to accompany Father Júlio Aço
on excursions into the outskirts of Díli to offer extreme
unction to the dying. Secretly, I noted that he remained
immune to happiness.

Happiness was too enamoured of my colleague Victor
Gândara, whom I considered the ideal priest. Happiness
was full of Victor's name when Venâncio arrived. The
government had never given out so many scholarships in
one year. It was profligate with what it had saved over
the years. Timor continued to follow to the letter a

policy of small economies. Happiness went off to Lisbon to study medicine on the same plane as myself and others who had been given scholarships. On a Swissair flight chartered for Portuguese soldiers, who, weary of long-drawn-out sea crossings, wanted to get home quickly. The sea was an antiquated affair suitable only for those mad navigators who had once set sail across the oceans in search of other lands and people, perhaps in search of themselves. When I said goodbye, I saw my parents' faces; they looked as content as if they had dispatched a parcel to some safe, distant destination. Afterwards, when they turned their backs on me, they embraced and wept.

I had seen photos and documentaries of the white city flooded with sunlight, pigeons and red rooftops. I expected to find a sea of people filling the streets with flowers and colours. It was a cold, overcast, rainy Sunday when we landed. An October in a wintry autumn. The avenues were empty, apart from a few scattered figures dressed in black. I remembered Amália then and went to bed so that when I woke up, I could go in search of that river where the people all went to wash away the sorrows that rose up to me from the street in the voice of another singer, Adriano Correia de Oliveira:

'*Tejo que levas as águas . . .*'

Tagus bearing away the waters . . .

8

Gradually I came to accept the idea that the airport in Timor was just an overgrown field; not only an airfield, but a field that served various purposes. The plane was an iron bird that would land now and again and frighten the goats, pigeons and grasshoppers. And when it landed, it was a monstrous, noisy, propeller-driven thing that scorched the grass and only ever carried very important people. You heard the engines first, a roar that almost lifted the roof off the school and made the mat covering the dirt floor ripple like a flying carpet. When I ran outside to see it, the plane's wings would be catching the sun, glittering like a starry bird skimming the surface of the sea. Then the VIPs – civil, military and religious – would descend, as if from the heavens. And I would try to work out which one had the most God-like face.

By now, I had been to Lisbon airport several times to meet some distant relative or other who had, with the outbreak of civil war, fled first to Australia, which was like a warehouse that would later return to the original Portuguese sender what was to them an expendable cargo. Those in whom I had placed my trust, the horsemen of the apocalypse, excluded from clerical tasks and turning to lay activities, had in the end been unable to avoid the bloody war that broke out between brother parties. Words were silenced by the music of guns and by fixed bayonets. Fratricide as destiny, and the Biblical surrender to fate as told in ancient tales.

Most of the arrivals were civil servants. They came to claim the funeral allowance due not to them but to East Timor. With the end of the imperial age, they were finally given leave of absence – forcibly exiled to a homeland some had never been to before. I could not find a close relative to embrace and thus weep out my accumulated grief for the dead and for the misfortunes of those survivors who had been abandoned for ever to the mercies of fate – on both sides of the frontier. I found out later that my father had been imprisoned by the independence-fighters of Fretilin. It was partly his fault for being a supporter of the UDT. In the absence of most of his party who had crossed the border, he who had once been entrusted with saving lives was paying for himself, for them and for no one. That is the fate of the unfortunate.

Others suffered a worse fate. Like Abel, dying a bloody death at the hands of a brother.

I did not go to the airport to meet those who arrived from the wrong side of the border, stripped of dreams. Indonesia was returning the orphans to their stepmother having first, in the name of the children, killed the birth

mother whom Fretilin had proclaimed to be the true
mother. At first, along with the successive waves of
people from Africa, they were described as *retornados* –
returnees. Returnees from Timor. Then came the expul-
sions from East Timor and, as more was learned about
the drama of the independence fighters dying in the
mountains of Timor, that wave of rejects was rejected by
those who had been dislodged by the Indonesian invasion and left to bemoan their own guilt. Having shaken
off their part of the blame for the fate met by those who
had stayed, the exiled political elite of the UDT kept a
safe distance from the scholarship holders, whom they
considered to be red guards, plunderers of past and present. They recognized, however, that in East Timor it was
the *maubere* who for the moment was working best on
the ground, given the helicopter-loads of Indonesian
corpses flown out from the occupied territory, corpses
which they silently counted. As for the future, they
hoped that in time, once this period of expiation and
purging was over, the Timorese would recover their true
nature and their land.

To tell the truth, I was afraid to go anywhere near
Vale do Jamor, where the refugees were housed. They
had seen bloody deaths, their own side had killed and
been killed. Common sense told me that a wounded
animal heals its wounds by sharpening its claws. I feared
for my own skin.

I was living in a students' residence in an area of Lisbon near the river. An aristocratic place that harboured a nest of future managers, who at the time, though, were still reading the Marxist primer. They were young men from various parts of Portugal, from the autonomous regions and from the new Portuguese-speaking African countries. It was like living with ghosts straight out of my school books. We knew all about each other's country without ever having been there. We knew each other through the past. Although they all lamented my fate, I myself nursed the hope that I would be touched by some marvel, a hope like that shining in the eyes of the workmen who frequented the bar where I ate my soup, as they ordered a glass of brandy and put their X on their pools coupon. I regained the remembered paradise of childhood, which grew in strength inside me with each day that passed, so much so that it became the country I was exiled from, not Timor. I would have liked to cross the river and see Lisbon from the other side each morning and each evening. But it was not yet time to make the crossing – whenever Venâncio had talked about Charon and the Styx, he always spoke of it as the last possible resort, and then only after an unhappy love affair. I declined invitations from friends who promised me lively, crowded, sublime parties, fiestas, olive harvests and pig-roasts, while I waited for the 'revelation' which I felt sure was about to happen right on my street corner. And as time passed and nothing happened, I decided to go in search of the apparition.

I caught the morning train to the place which I had always been told was the centre of the universe: the railway junction at Entroncamento. There all the trains on earth met and crossed, carrying men of different races, from the north and the south, crusaders and Muhammadans. These were fantasies I had carried with me through time, on my peregrinations through the missionary schools. I closed my eyes so as not to be distracted by the landscape on the way to the earth's central point nor by the prophetic presence of migrant birds. I wanted to be surprised. When the train came to a halt and the loudspeakers announced the end of the line and a change of trains, I opened my eyes. We were in an empty station, full of hot metal tracks that burned beneath the train, which slept on the line like a dead boa constrictor. I asked where all the other trains were and all the different people who should be there, shouting, weeping, embracing, loving, killing and dying. It should have been the place where, for better or worse, men revealed what they were capable of. In the name of God and all His symbols. But it was like a desert, a silent, abandoned place where the remnants of empire were slowly dribbling away. And when no one answered me, I went to ask the station master where we were.

'Entroncamento,' he said, not even looking at me.

'Entroncamento?' I asked again, not believing what I was seeing.

Hearing my dazed and disappointed voice, and as if guessing the purpose of my visit there, he said with a mocking smile, 'What did you expect? If you came here in search of magic, you should have gone to Fátima. That's where all the miracles happen.'

When I didn't move, confirming the impression that I was in search of some strange phenomenon, he began to leave, and then asked, 'Where do you come from, then?'

'From Timor,' I said.

'Oh, we get lots of people from there. Now that everything's changed, they come here in search of a blessing and find they've ended up at the wrong shrine! I've never been to Africa myself, but I had a cousin who went there.' He paused, searching for the name of the place and taking as long about it as if he were following the original route of the caravels. At last, he opened his eyes wide, blinked as if defeated by the mists of time, and said with a shrug, 'I don't rightly know if it was Angola or Mozambique, not that it really matters. But he arrived back home barefoot!' he concluded, as if acknowledging the supremacy of fate.

He fell silent, regretting the loss of his cousin's shoes in Africa. I said nothing about the magic I had lost somewhere. I bought my ticket back to Lisbon, convinced that I would settle down by the river and wait for the right moment to make the crossing.

Whenever reality killed one of my illusions, it was immediately replaced by another, like a bead on a rosary. I used to walk by the river at the hour when others were leaving the city, especially if it was raining and the square was empty. I would watch the path followed by people leaving their offices and heading for home where their domestic duties awaited them. I was not bound by routine, but I longed for it. In the end, war, heroism and betrayals were all extreme acts carried out in order to attain precisely that kind of normality. Remaining on the outside could only lead to madness.

I sat down on the Quay of Columns, which I had always thought was called the Quay of Colons, at the spot which I judged to be the likely stopping place of those two eels my grandfather told me about, who would doubtless have travelled in the wake of the caravels, following the scent of the sandalwood. I dreamed of the day when they would lift up their heads and come to my hands, expecting me to give them eggs as my grandfather used to do with the eels in the spring. I always carried eggs in my pockets, ready. The lights from the quay lit up the waters and reflected the glimmer which I imagined to be the eyes of my river creatures. The boats sped past, indifferent, carrying sleeping travellers, like extras in a film about weary lovers and exhausted dancers.

Someone tapped me on the shoulder. I did not turn round, thinking it was probably another chap asking for a cigarette. Despite all the other people around, I was bound to be the chosen target. I had given my last packet to a tramp, thus avoiding being a glow-worm in the dark, his need was greater than mine. Another star in the firmament or simply a walking traffic light marking the stops for those furious days spent in search of nothing. But this time, someone had actually placed his hands on my shoulders, heavy hands smelling of rain and Balibó tobacco. I turned round. I met a pair of eyes like the eyes of the eels in the mud at the bottom of the river. For a startled moment, I thought I had before me a transmogrification of those submarine creatures.

'My name's Domingos,' he said, to calm me. 'And this is Mali Mau,' he added, indicating his companion with a glance. 'We've just come from Trafaria, we've got work there on a building site, and now we're going back to Odivelas. Let's go to that café over there.'

He took me by my right arm and dragged me through the crowd hurrying towards the quay; the mist and the smoke from the chestnut-seller concealed the boat so that the people vanished behind him as if they were hurling themselves into the water.

We sat down in the café and waited to be served. Domingos was strong and stocky; he had a round face and a constant smile – one of those people who hid their tears that way. Mali Mau was thin, ramrod straight, and looked at me with intent, distant eyes. They clearly expected me to introduce myself. But I said nothing. Domingos got up and went over to the waiter, who had shown no desire to come to our table. He touched the waiter with his right hand, to calm the beast. The waiter looked down at his white shirt, brushed at it with his hands and said, 'What do you want?'

'Tea!' said Domingos almost pleadingly.

'*Tea?*' said the waiter, astonished, glancing at the neighbouring table where some fur-coated ladies, their faces plastered with powder, were leaving lipstick marks on the cups. 'Tea!' he said again, looking Domingos up and down.

He brought the tea, though, and Domingos picked up the pot and filled the three cups. Conscious of the scrutiny of the ladies in mink, he took great care not to spill a single drop on the table. Anyone would think we had been taking afternoon tea all our lives.

'We live in Odivelas. Just near here . . .'

'Yes, I know it,' I said reassuringly.

In Timor everything was near. Time didn't matter, nor did distance, for however remote a place was, people would always tell you, 'It's just over there.'

'Where do you live?' he asked, trying to wipe the surprise from his face.

They had discovered me. I thought that time, cold and the change of latitude would have altered my face and my gestures, just like the civil servants who were allowed here on leave and would return home with the accent and airs of Lisbon. I was delighted to realize that my Afro hairstyle, copied from the Black Panthers, could not conceal the fact that I was the son of a *calades*.

'In Lisbon,' I said.

Domingos smiled. He understood my reluctance to shatter the shell of mystery I had built around myself. We drank our tea in silence and let our minds wander, stroking the hot cups. We each plunged into the past in order to discover each other's present.

In a desire to justify its image as a freedom movement that would regenerate ancestral values, Fretilin chose the *maubere*, the native Timorese, as the face of the new man and restored the word to its original native, pagan sense of 'brother'. The UDT thought that giving the people such a name meant stripping them of their dignity. They felt it was wrong to make a symbol of a word that the UDT itself used to designate the uneducated; they said it was like reclaiming a new man from an ancient race, stealing Rousseau's theory of the noble savage. But everyone knew that this word, made either mythical or offensive by the opposing parties, had both a past and a profile. Domingos and Mali Mau were the personification of the *maubere*, excluded from the benefits of Portuguese colonialism, an old man's face on the body of a child, barefoot and illiterate. They never had access to education, never read any schoolbooks, did not even know where Portugal was, could not speak the language, and, in the majority, despite all the missionaries' efforts, had not been baptized and were still immersed in pagan rites. So I wondered why they had come to Portugal, and if they had not, in fact, made the wrong choice. What were they doing in this country of which they knew nothing? I noticed that they were wearing jeans, leather boots and jackets with designer labels. They were dressed according to the age, looking like a combination of *maubere* and pop singer.

'Domingos what?' I asked.

'Just Domingos!' he said loudly and conclusively. 'My boss gave me the name.' He gulped down his tea in an effort to remember. 'I wanted to be baptized so that I could have a surname too. Perhaps Sávio like the saint. But the war messed up my baptism, and now I don't want a surname any more.'

'Boss?'

'Yes, the Chinese guy in Bobonaro.'

He looked at me, expecting me to say that I knew his boss in Timor. And when I didn't respond, he added, 'I was a *matroz*, an errand boy. I looked after his children. I'd wipe their bums and eat chow mein. Then I used to help the truck driver. I'd put the wedge under the wheel and turn the crank.' He made a turning gesture with his hand. 'The first trip I made to Díli, as the driver's mate, we got caught in the crossfire between the *malaes* who were escaping to Atambua and the *maubere* soldiers who were after them, one minute raising a clenched fist, the next squeezing the trigger. My boss had us turn round, and we didn't stop till we got to the border. So then I went to Atambua too. And when the Portuguese came to airlift out the others, they had to bring us as well.'

'The others?'

'Yes, the *malaes*, the civil servants and their families. They live in Vale do Jamor now.'

Mali Mau had still said nothing, but he was watching me intently. We had finished our tea, but the rain had begun to pound the city. The waiter cleared the tables and tidied chairs and then came and stood next to us with a bucket of soapy water and a broom in his hand, ready to kick us out. He stood tapping his foot and dripping water. He seemed to be saying: either you leave, or I'll tip this all over you. Domingos paid for the tea and grabbed me by the arm again, dragging me to the bus stop.

'We're going to Odivelas,' he ordered.

I hadn't even had a chance to reply before I was bundled onto a bus. As we crossed the city, I saw their calm faces pressed against the rain-spattered window, their shining eyes looking out for reference points from previous journeys. The other passengers left their seats at stops along the way, and the cold air that came in through the doors made my skin prickle as if some invisible being had come in through the window and sat down in the empty seats. When there were just the three of us left, looking at each other, at the driver, at the landscape outside, I finally realized that they were lost.

'This is the last stop,' said the driver, turning off the lights. 'Everybody off.'

We stepped out into a wasteland somewhere near Portela. To escape the rain we had just got on the first bus that came along, without knowing where it was going. As if impelled by some supernatural spirit wanting to play a joke on us, we had been taken to an unfamiliar spot by a driver who, in the confusion caused by the traffic and the storm, had been replaced by a ghost.

'This isn't Odivelas!' whispered Domingos.

'Rain-fila!' said Mali Mau, staring at the wasteland and then up at the sky in search of some star to steer by. And without a word, he removed his boots, took off all his clothes and stood there completely naked. Then he put everything back on again, this time the wrong way round, just like nature, in order to find the way home.

Domingos stared at him and immediately seized him by the arm before Mali Mau, possessed by some homing instinct, could be swept away by a breeze or a transient falling star. I went over to the driver, who was peering at us curiously through the window, armed with a stick in case anything even stranger should happen. I asked him the way to Odivelas and explained how the confusion had arisen. We got back onto the bus and when Mali Mau, now Mau Mali, showed his pass, the driver stared in astonishment at the back-to-front traveller. From the smile on his lips, it looked as if he were going to ask him for a pass with a matching back-to-front photo.

'These guys,' he said, shaking his stick, 'they're always back to front!' He gave a cruel laugh. 'That's why you can't see them in the dark,' he concluded by way of clarification.

Mali Mau held on to the banister so as not to bump his head on the stairs as we went up to the fifth floor of a building filled with the Brazilian accents of the latest TV soap, *Gabriela Cravo e Canela*. It was a building intended for those who had been turfed out of the colonies, for those who, once, as part of Portugal's much-vaunted 'multi-racial empire', had been a favourite topic in effusive speeches by colonial mandarins. The door stood open onto a tiny room crammed with four bunk beds in which slept six young men, mouths agape, indifferent to the charms of Sónia Braga on the posters decorating the walls. They were swaddled in voluminous blankets that covered their chest and belly, leaving exposed their hard, voluminous faces, adorned with large lips and strong teeth and dominated by the flat nose typical of the *calades*. Their large feet were drawn up, but you could still see their broad, spreading toes, like a hand of bananas, on which utilitarian shoes had left deep marks and calluses. I knew immediately that they were from the mountainous regions where they used to grow cassava, coffee and maize, but had been caught out by a *rain-fila* and been evicted from a place whose location they could not now recall even in dreams. Mali Mau immediately lay down on the upper bed of an empty bunk, without bothering to recompose the clothes he had reversed in order to find a lost path. Perhaps he thought that he had not yet found the right one and that only sleep could restore it to him. He went to bed with his eyes as red as if he had been fished out of the salty river. In his sleep, he thrashed about and snorted like a wild boar caught in a trap set for him by hunters. Domingos picked up his blanket and spread it out on the floor like a mat. He offered me his bed with its military green mattress darkened by time and the bodies that had lain on it; a burning cigarette end had left a veritable crater in the midst of the green pasture. He felt that my body was too sensitive for the concrete floor. The way he lay down parallel to my bed made him look like a guard. Domingos and Mali Mau had found me on their way back from work, like a buffalo far from the herd and whose owner they were vaguely trying to locate. In the meantime they felt they had a duty to take care of it, of me. I couldn't sleep for the smell of sweaty boots and the noisy concerto of their breathings. They seemed to be climbing mountains or digging deep down into their memories. I feared for their future, wondered how they would cope in this land, where they had been suddenly transported into the pages of Pigafetta, Magellan's chronicler, describing slaves brought by the caravels. I wanted to leave during the night, but cold, fear and the absence of public transport meant that I lay there without closing my eyes, trying to hunt down the news or the atrocities which they, in their dreams, kicked against. I hoped that in the morning, with their faces lit by the sun, I would be able to recognize one of my father's 'godchildren', who might be able to tell me his ill or good fortune.

When I woke up, however, they had all gone. There was only the warmth of absent bodies. The blankets on the beds smelled of sweat, damp and the musk-scented *laku*. They had left in the early hours before the sun rose, and the blanket on which Domingos had slept had been placed over my body. Had they been standing over me, trying to work out who I was? They were the people who in Timor would also have been up before cock-crow. Eternal early risers. I felt in my pockets for the sacred eggs intended for the eels sleeping in the mud of the Tagus. Hunger gripped my stomach, and I was considering committing an original sin by filching a gift intended for the gods. But nothing bad would happen to me, I was sure; after all, when I had been an altar boy, I used to eat the leftover hosts. I had to withdraw my hands at once, though, my fingers sticky with albumen. My trouser pockets were full of beaten egg that had left a damp stain all over my stomach. I was in no state to go out into the street. I grabbed a pair of designer jeans, which, I learned later, belonged to Nai Buti. The rest of the building, like a chicken house, was beginning to stir into life. Faces born in the landscapes of paradise peered from the windows, perhaps in search of the Portuguese sun, heat and beaches that had illustrated schoolbooks whose pages had been almost as brown as the tanned skins of holidaymakers.

Most of them I never saw again. They paid for their clothes, cigarettes and lovers with those early morning sallies. They expected no one's charity or compassion. Such feelings and such fees were not for the likes of that band of men scattered by the wind.

9

Finally, I decided to go to Vale do Jamor. An invitation from a colleague of my father's. It was Christmas, a season when no one harbours a grudge. After that, who knew. We did not talk about politics or about family members who had stayed behind in Timor. A pact sealed by the face turned to the television screen and by a beer in the hand. Sometimes we would mutter something between gritted teeth, and my host hoped that this would be the last real Christmas – cold and miserable. He longed for warmer Christmases, nearer the south, nearer Timor. All he needed was for some relative to get up the energy to write him a letter inviting him to longed-for, dreamed-of Australia.

There was not much *amor* about Vale do Jamor; there was instead the fetid smell from the river and the mud surrounding the canvas tents donated by the Red Cross. Most of its inhabitants were civil servants with links with the UDT. They hoped to get their papers processed and be reintegrated into civil service life, or else to take early retirement and make the kangaroo-leap over to Australia. The torment of their stay here was submerged in the hope of the El Dorado of the Southern Cross. After a period of adaptation, some were, in fact, taken back into the civil service and they left that vale of tears, tears which they dried elsewhere. Others, with fewer means, stayed on and took up the old habits of daily life in Díli – they planted gardens round some of the huts, and even raised cockerels, fighting cocks they said, to relive the excitement of betting at the weekly bazaar. It was felt, however, that this passion for cock-fighting should be restricted to the less violent colours, thus excluding the terrible *manu mean* – the red cockerel. The huts vacated by their inhabitants, emigrants or displaced persons, were immediately taken over by sporting clubs of a regional nature, under the influence of some charismatic personality. They would organize dances to celebrate baptisms or birthdays. Various football teams sprang up and took part in competitions with other local teams. They put on basketball tournaments for women. A children's choir, in Timorese dress, toured various venues in Portugal performing traditional songs and dances, and were even invited to perform at the Casino in Estoril before Princess Grace of Monaco. They went from being returnees to Portugal to refugees from the war and, although they kept up their Lusitanian patriotism with trips to castles and sacred places – vigils in monasteries dedicated to heroic deeds – they began to disseminate Timorese culture, invoking the drama of those dying in the mountains and of those who, before, had driven them over to the other side of the border, right into the claws of the giant lizards of Java. But Vale do Jamor was still an anti-*manu mean* zone, an anti-Fretilin zone, watched over more or less vigilantly by two missionaries.

One day Domingos, Mali Mau and Nai Buti turned up at the students' residence, without warning. They knew about me without my ever having told them anything. They had come to return my trousers and brought with them a pair of black shoes dangling from Domingos' fingers. Such a gift awoke an old presentiment – only the dead wear black shoes, even if they have gone barefoot all their lives.

'What size do you take?' Domingos asked me, throwing the said black shoes at my feet.

'You're not my angel of death I hope,' I said, joking. 'I don't like black shoes. When I die, I want to be barefoot the way I was born. Besides, I don't take size 42.'

Domingos picked up the shoes and said that perhaps big Inácio could use them instead. Nai Buti (which means Mr White) did not live up to his name. He was extremely dark. Perhaps they had given him that name to lighten his future. He gave me back my trousers, washed, and didn't even ask about his designer jeans. They sat down on my bed, and Domingos, although he couldn't actually play the guitar, picked mine up and clumsily picked out a Timorese dance tune on the strings. The other two sang along and encouraged me to join in. I got what remained of a bottle of brandy out of the cupboard and the singing continued until we ran out of songs, and Domingos announced, 'We're forming a cultural group!'

'A what?' I said, surprised.

'A cultural group. Performing *maubere* songs and dances.'

That was the first time I had heard a genuine *maubere* – a *maubere* through and through – declare himself. They had adapted more successfully than I had, just as buffalo can live happily on dry land or wet. My idea of culture, formulated through knowledge acquired in rooms lined with fat, heavy tomes, was profoundly shaken by the ostentatious way in which Domingos, an illiterate, uttered the word 'cultural'. They had a request to make too. That little rehearsal in my room was a disguised invitation to join their group. They said I could recite a few poems, not by any of those nostalgic, reactionary, colonialist poets, but by our own revolutionary writers.

And so, one weekend evening, I presented myself before the then Fretilin-elected minister of the Democratic Republic of East Timor, Abílio Araújo, who presided over the forum that would decide whether or not to include me. It was my second encounter with that overly gifted

man who had once thought he would share the administration of the Portuguese territory with Mário
Carrascalão and it was to him that I had to address my
self-criticism for my bourgeois, decadent past and my
counter-revolutionary experiences. It was the same
method they used to use at the seminary for public con-
fessions during retreats. Judging from his slightly
Gioconda-like smile when I finished my piece, he was
doubtless also reminded of this. I promised to follow his
example. There was no penance. But that enigmatic smile
weighed like a ton of rosaries. I was admitted to that
community of *mauberes* trained for cultural missions –
and for military ones too, although I still don't quite know
what those were, whether they would take place in
Mozambique (where, according to the minister, a treach-
erous faction of Fretilin was holed up), or involve crossing
the Timor sea in a pedalo submarine that someone
dreamed of building. It was a time when, given the siege
of silence surrounding any news from the interior, we had
to out-dare each other. It was just as well that Timor was
not depending on our exploits. They said that they could
rely only on their own forces, while we just mouthed
orders, unaware that the message of self-reliance was
actually addressed to those members of the Fretilin central
committee engaged in diplomatic missions outside Timor,
and who gradually faded from view.

While others nurtured the dream of building a

handcrafted submersible, we toured Portugal from north to south, from community to community, performing traditional Timorese dances, singing the Fretilin anthem, *Foho Ramelau*, and declaiming poems by Borja Costa. We were competing with Vale do Jamor's UDT cultural groups who were demanding proper citizenship rights for the Portuguese of the Far East. At the same time, in order to win over reluctant audiences, we revamped the old dances with music that would touch hearts and minds, and did whatever else we could to seduce the more susceptible elements, rewriting love songs to include evocative lines that spoke longingly of home and of those who had stayed behind. Vale do Jamor surrendered a little more with each dance, especially when the party leaders, attracted by the prospect of a more rewarding life in Australia, abandoned their subjects to our mercies, to the red invaders. The sad fate of all subjects! We were introduced to the Minister of Defence, another ex-seminarian and a former tenor, as well as a super-fit, long-distance runner, who, in between revolutionary songs, would dust off his artistic gifts and sing, in a nostalgic, tremulous voice, ballads from the seminary in Dare – once a Dare student, always a Dare student, whispered a colleague, a convinced ex-seminarian himself. But I noticed that the young man was becoming visibly weighed down beneath ministerial responsibility. Dispatched on a mission abroad to drum up practical support, he had made himself a champion of the cause in various corners of the globe, where nothing much happened apart from receptions with a lot of marching and fanfares. Thus, troubled, he sought comfort in the hymns he used to sing when he was a believer and used his vocal talents in praise of the Almighty.

But the memory of those musical days did not distract me from the fact that I was there in the presence of ministers from East Timor. Essentially, they represented an alternative lay altar, but an altar none the less, since all seminarians had been educated for the pulpit. Freed from the obligation to save the souls of pagans, they now had the no less important task of saving the skins of the *mauberes*. To avoid any misunderstandings – just in case the Devil should start weaving distorted comments – and under pressure to do something concrete, the Minister of Defence immediately struck a ministerial pose and re-formed the cultural *mauberes* into a military squad wearing emblems copied from the colonial armed forces. All that was needed now was to make the crossing. No one had heard anything more from the naval architect. The news being circulated at the time spoke of Indonesian victories and, on the ground, the Indonesian army's besiege-and-destroy campaigns were proving brutally effective, culminating in the death of Nicolau Lobato, brother of the Minister of Defence, who was on leave of absence from the front line, both of them sons of the much-missed Master Narciso from Soibada.

It was the end of 1978. The power struggle in the governmental ranks outside Timor, with everyone trying to out-*maubere* everyone else in order to claim an exclusive mandate, left its marks inside Timor. A high official unburdened himself in Tetum to the effect that each person should seek his own path – *ida idak buka nia dalam*.

Thus ended the time of dreaming. Looking for a way forward for each of us, we went for a walk by the river on the first day of 1979. Domingos confided that his Chinese boss, installed in Australia, had suggested that he join him there. He wouldn't go back to being a mere *china-atan* – the servant of a Chinese businessman – because the boss's son had been killed in the invasion. Mali Mau said nothing and just kept staring at the river where a sheet of newspaper bobbed on the water. He fished it out as if it contained a message from the other side of the ocean. He said it was about Timor, even though he didn't know how to read. It did, in fact, carry a small item about the death of Nicolau Lobato. Mali Mau made a boat out of the sodden paper, blew on it and returned it to the river where it succumbed to the rough waves stirred up by the ferries. He came and sat down beside me. He dried his tears and launched into a long story, which he said he had never told to anyone else, but which came back to him again and again in dreams from which he woke drenched in sweat, as if he had been swimming in the depths of the river.

'When my mother was pregnant with me, she used to say that she wanted a good future for her child. She tried to find out from wealthy people how they came by their fortune, but when they spoke only of inheritances, natural talents and suchlike, she gave up. Then one day, an old woman came to her and told her that, if fate smiled upon her, she might accidentally meet the spirit of seduction, Pontiana. My mother didn't believe in chance, though, and so prepared herself just in case. Every night, she would sit outside the house next to the old *gondoeiro* tree where she imagined Pontiana lived. She protected herself with the scent of flowers and sandalwood and left a clay pot full of water to act as a mirror to attract the spirit. She thought that, like all seducers, Pontiana was bound to be vain and wouldn't be able to resist peering into the pot of water to look at herself or to wash her face before getting dressed up to seduce some errant young man. Her vigil, however, was often disturbed by the arrival of owls, and, being superstitious, she made a fire and scared off the noisy intruders with fiery brands. Sometimes, my father would demand that she come and lie down beside him on their sleeping-mat. And he used to say that, if she didn't, he would have an account to settle with Pontiana. Many moons passed and that prolonged waiting meant that my mother, while growing big with me, was gradually becoming thinner and thinner. Just as I saw the light of day and gave my first yell, she uttered her last sigh and was snuffed out in the darkness. My father buried her next to the *gondoeiro* tree, promising to avenge himself on the spirit. When he tried to cut the tree down, he saw my mother's face in the middle of the whirling leaves and he pursued the wind that raced across the fields and which sowed misfortune and destruction. He did this so often that he became known by the other farmers as the storm thief. They waited a long time and worked out which day he would make his next crossing of a particular valley through which the wind passed. The members of the two main houses arranged themselves at the entrance. They said he would doubtless be tired. As the storm passed, they tightened a rope across the pass and he fell to the ground. With his bristling mane of hair, he looked like a wild horse, slavering and panting, expelling the air accumulated over the half millennium he had spent in pursuit of my mother's spirit. When we buried my father, the two houses that had joined forces to trip him up got into an argument over the ownership of the rope. Each claimed exclusive rights. Driven out of the village, the members of the Kaibauk house took refuge in the cave of a large lizard which immediately promised them reparation. And so it was that my village, at that time dominated by the members of the Nakroma house, was put to the torch. I wandered far and wide and I ended up here, as if I had risen up from the depths of the river. That's why I feel this constant dampness inside me.'

'Look, I'm breathless, just like your Dad,' I said as if my words could comfort him for the pain overflowing his bony ribcage.

Mali Mau opened his hands and stood barechested, throwing off his bonds, to feel the cool air blowing along the corridor formed by the Quay of Columns.

'I'm going to stay right here!' he said, indicating the equestrian statue of Dom José.

Even today, he walks around the Baixa, circling the statue and the horse, sitting on the quay, mingling with the sellers of bracelets, leather goods, ornaments and dreams. He has let his hair grow long like Bob Marley, but his small body and light, easy step mark him out as having the soul of a *maubere*. Sometimes he helps António in celebrating the ritual of the man-statue. He sits on the ground, like his mother, and relives the long wait for the spirit to come and give him a fortunate future.

António stretches forward when he hears the clink of a coin, and the voice of the rasta sings amongst the columns, 'No woman, no cry!'

10

My family told me that he had meanwhile returned from the bush. It wasn't really a return. Rather, he had been restored alive to the city. I would never have imagined he could withstand such hardship. As a child, I had watched him, when ill, take a syringe and inject himself in the buttock with penicillin. Like an animal licking a wound, expecting no help from anyone. But as he grew older and with the continuing lack of news, I began to have serious doubts. The thought of him wandering in the elements through the bush meant that, with each day that passed, my hopes of his being found alive diminished. My mother preferred not to wear mourning in case she invoked ill luck. When he turned up in the town of Liquiçá, they told me at once. He became my hero. Not for any heroic deeds or his dedication to the cause, but because he had survived both. Especially after the stories told by those who had suffered the misery of guerrilla warfare and the malice of the Indonesian army, and who were later rehabilitated by what had once been the mother country but was subsequently demystified as the land of the colonizer and, ultimately, the land of welcome, thanks to the Red Cross programme for reuniting separated families. They were reunited through the old colonial ties that the erstwhile mother country still granted her former subjects, even though the umbilical cord had been cut in such a way as to make the child bleed and the mother grieve.

I went to the airport to meet him. This time I was sure I would find a relative to embrace. He was accompanied by his family – his support. No one cried, either because their tears had all dried up, or because their hearts felt that they should reserve that humanizing liquid for another occasion. He embraced me almost absently. I did not feel the hot blood that once used to swell the veins in his head when he would return, sweating, on horseback, having gone to save the life of some patient in a distant village, and, glad to be back home, take me on his knee and rock me to sleep. Before embarking for Lisbon, he seemed to have emptied out onto the earth every drop of that red fluid of life, as if he himself knew the real reason he had come, beneath the official explanation of recovering his memory, lost after a stroke. He had brought with him that native, pagan spirit, inconstant and rebellious, which sometimes withdrew, leaving him to wander aimlessly in time, until it returned with its accustomed weight and authority. He seemed delighted with the long journey through the air on that transcontinental flight. I had to think back in order to understand this. I remembered my childhood, when, after the crossing between Díli and Ataúro, I was unable to stand and fell to the ground, still rocked by the rhythm of the waves but pleased to be back on dry land. I was sure that once he had recovered from the journey he would sift slowly through what remained of his memory for some recollection of this land which he had once urged on me as our true home when it came to conjugation of verbs, arithmetical sums and geography, and which all travelled along railway lines terminating at Entroncamento. He had been in the habit of reading a large Portuguese dictionary, and I thought that the words, blackened by all the tumult, would gradually rise into the light again, all linked together. But the time he had spent in the bush had made him lose his grasp on vocabulary. When he spoke, he would pad out sentences with words from various of the indigenous tongues he had learned as a nurse to decipher the malarial conditions hiding behind the languages of his patients. Sometimes, he would dredge up the English gleaned from the Australian commandos in the Second World War. His amnesia allowed him access only to the memories he did not need. He would greet passers-by, thinking they were relatives or former patients, and when they did not respond, he would say he couldn't understand how people could have such short memories, how they could forget so easily. Enraged, he would yell at them, 'Communists!'

But he never seemed disappointed. He suffered rather from the lack of space, hemmed in by the four walls of a social security boarding house. From time to time he would disappear, explaining later that he had gone off into the bush. To breathe. In fact, he went down to the railway station to watch the trains leaving for such destinations as Maubisse, Tutuala, Balibó and others whose names he alone knew. Time passed and with it the hope that he would remember what had happened to him and be able to savour the reality of Portugal, images of which he had so often seen in my schoolbooks.

Under Portuguese administration, as a civil servant, he could have made use of the much sought-after leave of absence. He had never even considered it, occupied as he was with the everyday business of looking after his numerous children and patients. He would sometimes complain that it was really intended for people originally from Portugal or for those with family ties with Europe. He was rewarded with aspirin, to cure the pain of remaining on the far side of the cape of storms. And when I got headaches at exam time, he taught me to chew the pills so that they would take effect more quickly.

Now he brought with him the papers he had managed to get together to deal with his reintegration and his pension rights, so that he could take a trip around Portugal, the real country. When I reminded him of that possibility, he told me that he had seen it all before and felt no desire to travel those roads and visit those places again. What he wanted back were the bush paths. He heard about the deaths of friends and acquaintances, old men like him, who in fleeing from the storm in their own land had died in the cold of winter or the drought of summer. He did not go to their funerals. Not because he did not want to. The family wanted to save him the *via dolorosa* that might one day be his. Not the body's repose in death, but the giving of the flesh to the earth upon burial and the gathering together of the bones at the cemetery. Seeing the earth dug and redug a thousand times. I thought about the fate of those old men who had crossed continents, escaping a violent death only in order to die an old man's death, without even the right to have a white gum tree or grass growing on their grave. Like the buffalo swept by flood waters from the banks of the Carau-ulum to be buried in the mud of the estuary that drains out into the *tassi mane*, the calmer seas to the north of East Timor, known as the Male Sea.

Once the reintegration process was over, he decided to get a room of his own on the other side of the Tagus, by the cloudy, spacious waters of Miratejo, so as to enjoy a unique view of the city that had once been the capital of the empire. A cheap house, a cramped cage, as the sole legacy of all he had accumulated since his days at the school in Soibada: the Japanese invasion, his travels round the island as a nurse, imprisonment during the civil war, as well as his long vigil in the bush during the guerrilla war. Having found a resting place, he could finally go to the parties belatedly celebrating the endless reconciliations between the Timorese political rivals in exile, who promised to respect each other and to wear less aggressive colours. Pinker reds and almost sky-blue blues.

An old man would come and visit our family now and then. He lived a long way away, he had to catch a train, then a boat, then a bus. He wasn't in a hurry. He walked as if he were the master of time. That must be the only compensation life gives to the old. He had the slow gait of buffaloes walking through mud, and the suffering, sacrificial gaze of animals kept as pets or as part of *estilu*, the traditional consecration ceremonies. He would ring the bell, then come up the stairs to the first floor, removing his hat and using it to wipe the sweat from his face, greeting my parents in Tetum. Then he would sit down, his camera still slung round his neck. While he recovered his breath, he would remark that at the school in Soibada, the people from Ataúro were always the best swimmers. He would emphasize the name 'Soibada' in order to instil authority and to arouse my respect.

He was Master Alberto, the only old man to visit my father. He had come to Portugal after the invasion and now spent his time capturing moments for posterity. He visited the houses of fellow Timorese refugees, re-establishing old links and acting as a bringer of news and other truths. He had made several pilgrimages to the Holy Land and similar shrines. He brought with him photos of those places and told stories about them, lingering longer over some than over others. My father would stare distractedly up at the ceiling wanting to show his own photographs, the ones he kept behind his eyes, unable to get at the negatives. They both wanted to show off the trophies brought back from their wanderings. They would have lunch and discuss distant, disappeared friends. Master Marçal, Master Quintão, a nursing colleague and many others. In the middle of these accounts, their eyes would occasionally fill with tears which they would disguise by saying that it was time for a few photographs for posterity. They would take it in turns to stand by a piece of furniture, which served as a plumb line, and to press the button on the camera. And since they both always forgot to put on their hats, leaving themselves unprotected, they would have to re-enact the scene, this time looking more composed. They would sit down again, glancing all around them, and, now and then, one would throw out a word as bait to reel in some juicy bit of conversation from the other. Suddenly they would both be talking at once, recounting different stories from the past. They only coincided when they talked about the war of Manufahi. Master Alberto, from the kingdom of Lacló, was loyal to the colonial authorities, and my father, a native of Manufahi, was loyal to Dom Boaventura. They both agreed that the *malae* was wrong to try to seduce the native queen. It was as if they wanted to be reconciled again over the war that put an end to the pacification campaigns. After almost a century, they were reliving the memory of what proved to be a landmark in Timor's history: the Manufahi rebellion and its subsequent suppression beneath the watchful eyes of the Portuguese Admiral Gago Coutinho, who, later, with Sacadura Cabral, made the first flight across the South Atlantic. The two of them had ancestors on opposite sides of the barricades. They would hum tunes from the old days which I assumed to be songs of encouragement to the troops. Just as suddenly they would fall silent and then they wore hard, sad, Lenten faces, and the shadows of evening would begin to seep into the apartment and wrap about them like an old blanket. And at that moment, their presence would point an accusing finger at the generation which I did not represent, but whose education and health they had tended: *What did you do to us, to yourselves, to the people we left alive and well in your hands?*

They would say goodbye and one would make his way back home, as would the other one, staring out at the dark night.

Sometimes I got the feeling that my father wanted to talk about what had happened in the bush. On the *maubere* radio I had heard news about the Indonesian campaigns and about the atrocities committed. He had been there and I longed to know the truth. Acts of heroism and betrayal, people dying and abandoned, suicides and murders. But he was travelling further back in time, avoiding my questions and mixing up the war against the Japanese with the war of Manufahi. When I tried to broach the subject of his painful experiences in the bush, he would shut up like a rock. Then he would weep silently. Like morning dew falling on stones.

People told me that he was brave and the possessor of a *matam-élic*, a charm that allowed him to change into different animals in order to elude the military: José Alexandre, the long-haired Académica goalkeeper, writer of sonnets and one-time seminarian at Dare. He was also Xanana Gusmão, the leader of the guerrilla war, firing the hearts of those in the mountains and the souls of the young people in the streets. I had seen photos of him, with the face of Che Guevara and in the pose of a prophet. Someone gave me a couple of his speeches, and all of them used the same rhetorical, literary language that my friend Venâncio used to use when he talked about Fernando Pessoa in the days before Pessoa was excised from his cultural heritage. Even so, this new

resurgence did not make me question my distrust and
lack of belief in these ex-seminarian leaders. On the contrary. I feared that the appearance of a new luminary
could lead the people into mass extermination. Like
those prophets who carry their dreams to their conclu-
sion, dragging with them a multitude of desperate
followers. They never die alone. And Dare had already
provided other luminaries whose light had subsequently
dimmed, abandoning the people to darkness. But the
fact that they had forced the Indonesian soldiers to move
into the mountains in order to sign a ceasefire fuelled
hopes of better days. It put an end to that suicidal order:
Negotiate? Never!

Thanks to the Red Cross, the first young men began
to arrive from Timor and could show their wounds and
the marks of torture. They kept mentioning, almost *ad
nauseam*, the name of the commander of the guerrilla
war, as if they were the representatives of the prophet in
the mountains. They imitated their leader's political
speeches and, in their innocence, even tried to imitate the
poet's linguistic tics and tricks and got so tangled up in
words and ideas that they could find no way out of their
own intricately woven rhetoric. They spoke a Portuguese
that was sometimes classical, sometimes pure Díli
dialect. For them, language became an instrument of
combat. They weren't interested in how it was
constructed. Denouncing the genocide being practised

by the Indonesian army in Timor was far more important than grammar. They were, above all, missionaries
for the cause. Like those wilful Dominicans who disembarked one day in Timor and crossed the island in search
of pagans in order to spread the word of God, denounce
the slavery of the soul and promise a heavenly paradise.
They came to win back the incredulous supporters of
whom I was one. More than that, they wanted to win
back the mother country who, wearing veil and garland,
had sat down at the groaning table of Europe, which she
had once left to discover far-off lands and give birth to
rebellious orphans and emancipated children, and was
now savouring her return with candle-lit suppers, reliving her glorious past and bold deeds as depicted in
Brazilian TV soaps. A mother enchanted with the performance of her first-born. But those young men were
determined to carry out their mission. The raised fist
was replaced by the sign of the cross, and the revolutionary songs by prayers before political meditations. It
was as if they wanted to prove once and for all the existence of a people who shared the same beliefs and the
same language, but whose tragedy had been forgotten. A
new crusade by the children of the Discoveries who had
followed the caravel route back home. They said that the
children should not have to pay for the sins of the
fathers. And that their fathers should never bury the
hope that had been reborn from the ashes, thanks to

that new prophet called Xanana Gusmão.

I made several attempts to talk to my father about this living legend, in whom I had once placed all hope of saving the honour of my family, represented by my brother who played left back and, outwitted by the dangerous forward João Metan, had been sent sprawling while I closed my eyes in shame and kept them closed because the claque was celebrating a goal for the reds, and the goalkeeper, who would later be known as Xanana Gusmão, was lying spreadeagled on the ground.

My father never mentioned his name. He was afraid that saying it might break the charm. This was what he had always done. When he traversed rivers, he did not call out the name of the creature that lived there, the crocodile. When he crossed the sea, he never invoked the name of the master of the coral-rich waters, the shark. He thought he was still in the middle of a long crossing, that men needed a *rain-nain* or lord of the earth to watch over their paths. That is what happened in the war of Manufahi with Dom Boaventura. Dare had been bombed, but had covered itself once more with its roof of shining tin, with its writer of sonnets. My hopes grew then of returning to the island of Ataúro, as I had once promised the old steersman I would.

II

It was the eleventh time he had got lost. When the
police brought him back, they said it wasn't their job to
rescue people who were lost in time. His clothes were
sweaty and damp, sticking to his skin like the clothes of
a drowned man. His hair was long and dishevelled, his
beard thick and white, like that of a *bé-nain* or spirit of
the waters. After some days of seclusion to recover the
energy expended searching for a lost relative in a place
he said was called Betano, the light coming in through
the window restored his sense of direction. When he got
up, he couldn't stand and dropped to the floor. But his
eyes were distant. Looking somewhere to the south.
After several attempts, he regained his balance and his
centre. Having reconstructed for himself his house in
Manufahi, he asked me to take him back to the beach at
Betano. It was there that the Australian ships had
moored in order to take away the refugees during the
Japanese occupation. He wanted to save the buffalo he
had seen in dreams being swept along by the waters of
the Carau-ulum river that flowed out there before they
became the sea, in a recovery vessel sent especially by

former Australian soldiers. He looked for his box of syringes, left behind somewhere in Timor, that he had so often used to save patients' lives. He leaned on me at first, then walked independently, without his crutches. From the Ponta do Mato beach, in Seixal, he could see the city of Lisbon, which, at low tide, seemed nearer. He told me how sad he was not to have found the relative he had been looking for. And he had gone to Betano especially to find him. He would walk a few steps, then stop, his eyes scanning the beach. The distant shapes of the ferries reminded him of the rescue ship. And he took a white handkerchief out of his pocket and waved, so that they would know he was there. The dead fish left behind by the retreating tide lay intact on the sand. With no one to eat them, they were swimming onto dry land. He picked them up, one by one, and put them back in the water. He was not trying to restore them to life. He knew they were dead. As a former nurse, he had a very clear idea about what death was. The river was behaving like time, discarding the weakest ones along its shores. It simply horrified him to see something dying out of its natural element. He used to say that the only benefit the earth gets from its children is when they die. They always return what they took from her. When he considered his task over, he walked down across the beach and into the waters. However loudly I shouted, he did not hear me. He was crossing the river on foot, heading for the white city lit by the sun. When rescued by the cockle-catchers, he explained that someone had been calling to him from the other side. With a giant mirror. That the rescue ship had come to the wrong shore.

And he to the wrong river.

Then the longed-for letter of invitation came from Australia. At his request I took him an English dictionary. He intended to brush up on the language he had learned from the *malae-matam-balanda* – the foreigner with pale eyes. But his memory, so prodigal in restoring to him things he did not require, resisted giving him convenient access to the words. He would get irritated and grind his teeth with rage, punch the air, making moves he had learned in the art of *silat*, cursing in Mambae. But the hot, dry days of June soon made breathing difficult for him. Afraid that he would miss this unique opportunity, he wanted to catch an earlier flight. He felt that he had a mission in Australia, the collection of an old debt. He had his hair cut very short, shaved off his beard and bought a new suit. He was dressed like a collector not of taxes but of history. He went into Lisbon to get his passport photos taken. Two different ones, in contrary poses, as if of his front and his back. The point of departure and the end of the journey. When he returned, he could not climb the stairs to the first floor. He waited on the ground floor for the ambulance to come. The repetitive siren announced the end of the dream. In his hospital room, he tried spelling out to me the garbled names of Australian soldiers. He delegated his task to me. He wanted fate to finish the plot: *mate-bandera-hum*. A white sheet, like a flag bereft of colours and symbols, covered his bare, brown body. Ready to take the road back up Mount Cabalaqui. Death restored his motto to him. The spell he had been under was nothing but a *rain-fila*.

In the streets of Lisbon, the jacaranda trees were blooming as if nature had never lost its memory for colours. Like flaming torches, they kept vigil over the songs of the lorikeets, the *cacoaques* and all the other wounded birds, in the season when the coral tree flowers.

GLOSSARY

Apodeti – Timorese Popular Democratic Association; in favour of integration with Indonesia.

beiro – canoe in the form of a catamaran.

belak – A silver or gold circular ornament, worn on the chest.

bibere – native Timorese woman (the female version of *maubere*).

bunak – person from the Bobonaro region of East Timor.

cacoaque – species of cockatoo.

calades – a people living in central East Timor, mainly speaking *mambae*.

cipaio – an African soldier from one of the Portuguese colonies employed in the Portuguese army.

corocora – coaster or small ship engaged in coastal commerce.

dagadá – someone from the region of Los Palos in East Timor.

fado – a traditional Portuguese song form, usually full of yearning for what has been lost.

firaku – someone from the easternmost point of East Timor and a speaker of *macassae*.

Fretilin – Revolutionary Front for an Independent East Timor; in favour of a completely independent nation of East Timor.

korem-metam – a party held one year after the death of friend or relative.

kuda-ulum (pl. *kuda-uluns*) – 'horse-eaters'; pejorative term used to describe people from the Bobonaro region of East Timor.

laku – the palm civet, commonly found in coffee plantations; the musk produced by its anal glands is used in perfumery.

liurai – traditional local Timorese ruler.

Loro Monu – 'where the sun sets'; used to describe the western half of East Timor.

Loro Sae – 'where the sun rises'; the eastern half of East Timor.

macassaes – Timorese from the region of Baucau.

malae – a foreigner.

malae bá ona – 'the foreigner is leaving'.

malae oan – son of a white (Portuguese) foreigner.

malae-metam – an African.

mambae – the language spoken by the Mambae, one of the poorest hill peoples in East Timor.

manu-aman – cockerel.

manu mean – red cockerel; used by UDT supporters to describe members of Fretilin.

mate-bandera-hum – literally, 'to die in the shadow of the Portuguese flag'; the slogan of the pro-Portuguese UDT.

maubere – a mambae word meaning 'friend'. It was used by Portuguese to mean 'backward' or 'primitive', but reclaimed by Fretilin as symbol of the Timorese struggle against poverty and colonial subordination. To be a *maubere* was to be a son of East Timor.

Pontiana – the spirit of seduction.

rain-fila – a trick the land plays on intruders to make them lose their way; the only way to find the path home is to have one's guide remove all his clothes, put them on again back to front and then set off once more.

rain-main – spirit of the earth.

sikat – magical feather of an unusual colour, which is believed to mark out a winning fighting cockerel. The owner of such a bird would usually try to hide the feather from rival owners.

silat – a martial art practised in Malaysia and East Timor.

suku – originally a princedom, and later, under the Portuguese, an administrative unit.

tassi-fila – a trick the sea plays on intruders; see *rain-fila*.

UDT – Timorese Democratic Union; in favour of retaining old colonial links with Portugal.